The
Wrong Kind
of Different

Challenging
the Meaning of Diversity
in American Classrooms

The
Wrong Kind
of Different

Challenging
the Meaning of Diversity
in American Classrooms

Antonia Randolph

Teachers College, Columbia University
New York and London

The book is based on data collected as part of the Distributed Leadership Project that was funded by research grants from the National Science Foundation (REC-9873583) and the Spencer Foundation (200000039).

Published by Teachers College Press, 1234 Amsterdam Avenue, New York, NY 10027

Library of Congress Cataloging-in-Publication Data

Randolph, Antonia.
The wrong kind of different : challenging the meaning of diversity in American classrooms / Antonia Randolph.
    p. cm.
    Includes index.
    ISBN 978-0-8077-5384-2 (pbk. : alk. paper)
    ISBN 978-0-8077-5385-9 (hard cover : alk. paper)
        1. Multicultural education—United States. 2. Children of minorities—Education—United States. 3. Cultural pluralism—United States. I. Title.
    LC1099.3.R37 2013
    370.1170973—dc23   2012028217

ISBN 978-0-8077-5384-2 (paperback)
ISBN 978-0-8077-5385-9 (hardcover)

Printed on acid-free paper
Manufactured in the United States of America

20   19   18   17   16   15   14   13   8   7   6   5   4   3   2   1

Contents

Acknowledgments   **vii**

Introduction   **1**

Autobiography of a Name: The Perils of Color Blind Thinking   3

Organization of the Book   4

1. Dividing Up Difference   **7**

From Assimilation to Pluralism: A History of Race and
Ethnicity in Early 20th-Century American Schools   10

Racing Perceptions:
Disparate Teacher Perceptions of Minority Students   14

Consequences of Disparities in Teacher Perceptions of
Minority Students   15

From Pluralism to Assimilating Diversity:
Theorizing Laketown's Racial Orthodoxy   16

Laketown: Diversity East Coast Style   18

2. "I Admire Hispanic People":
Ethnic Credits and Racial Penalties in the Classroom   **23**

The Story of Difference: Race and Ethnicity as Narratives   24

Deserving and Undeserving Minorities:
Teachers' Ethnic and Racial Narratives   25

Well-meaning Cultural Tourists and Frustrated Natives   40

The Social Cost of Minority Status   41

3. Good and Bad Diversity:
Judging Difference in Multiracial Schools   **43**

A Multiracial Oasis in a Segregated City: Dodge and Bowen   44

"Lots of Flavor": The Attractions of Diversity for
Teachers at Multiracial Schools   46

How Teachers Came to Teach at Multiracial Schools 47

Giving Diversity Its Due: Performing Cosmopolitanism and Tolerance 48

Benefiting from Diversity: Productive Diversity and Multicultural Capital 53

Diversity's Discontents 58

Adding it Up: Balancing the Costs and Benefits of Diversity 61

4. "Kids Are Just Kids": Managing the Stigma Against Black Schools 63

Differences Beneath the Surface: Black Schools in Laketown 64

The Symbolic Burden of Teaching at Black Schools 65

"A Tough Place to Have Started":
First Experiences Teaching at Black Schools 67

The Heart of Darkness: The Concentrated Stigma of Black Schools 68

Coping with the Burden of Teaching Black 72

Responding to the Unique Needs of Black Schools 78

Adrift in the American Dream: How Diversity Left Black Schools Behind 84

5. Not Quite White: Preserving the White Norm 87

Not White 88

Not American 90

Not Mainstream 93

Not Middle Class 99

6. Fulfilling the Promise of Diversity 107

Orthodox Inequality: How Assimilating Diversity
Reinforces Social Hierarchies 109

Doing Diversity Differently 109

Appendix: Methodology 113

References 115

Index 119

About the Author 131

Acknowledgments

I could not have completed this project without the help of many people. Thanks to everyone with whom I worked on the Distributed Leadership Study: James Spillane, John Diamond, Amy Coldren, Jennifer Z. Sherer, Timothy Hallett, Frederick Brown, Loyiso Jita, Patricia Burch, and Richard Halverson. Thanks also to my mentors, Kerry Ann Rockquemore and Melissa Herman. Thanks to Pascha Bueno-Hansen, Tanya Saunders, Amy Steinbugler, Maggie Ussery, and Melissa Weiner for their willingness to read every draft with good humor and critical eyes intact.

More broadly, I enjoyed the support of the faculty at the University of Delaware, particularly Maggie Andersen, Ronet Bachman, Carol Henderson-Belton, Elizabeth Higginbotham, Susan Miller, and Ben Fleury-Steiner. Thanks to my family, especially my parents, James Randolph II and Cecilia Edwards-Randolph; my siblings, James Randolph III and Jacqueline Francis; and two very special aunts, Edith Randolph-Birney and Lupe Davidson. Thanks to everyone else who is unnamed, but not forgotten. Finally, thanks to my partner Dr. Anita M. Wells whose love and belief in me made it possible to finish. I could not have done it without all of you.

Introduction

A researcher asks a White teacher at a multiracial public elementary school to describe some of the strengths of the neighborhood where her school is located. She immediately replies, "It's really a diverse community. So it's really cool to be in a school like this because there are so many cultures represented." Across town, a Black teacher at a Black school explains that she did not like her current school at first, saying, "When I looked at it, I knew I wouldn't like it." This was especially true compared to the all-White school where she used to teach. She only decided to stay at the Black school after her sister told her that these "(S)tudents are different from the ones you worked with at your last job. You must realize that."

If we were to travel back to the 1950s and examine the same scenes, the White teacher may have viewed her school's diversity as a problem to be solved by assimilation, not an attraction. At the same time, the Black teacher may have seen teaching at an all-Black school as her duty, not a burden. A shift has occurred since the 1950s that has elevated teacher perception of some minority students, but not others. Hence, teachers can be drawn to a diverse school due to its diversity, while others can still rank Black schools as low status.

The scenes tell a complex story of how teachers respond to diversity in America today, in the wake of color blindness and multiculturalism. If teachers celebrate diversity, they cannot be accused of being biased against minority groups such as Blacks, that is, they cannot be racist. They can still claim color blindness. Yet, multiculturalism has not helped boost the status of Blacks. Teachers' praise of certain minority groups, due to multiculturalism, has allowed their negative perceptions of other minorities to stay unexamined. The two phenomena are connected.

This book is about a particular logic of diversity, one that elevates the status of multiracial schools and of certain minorities, but leaves the low status of Black schools and Black students intact. It is about the meaning of race and ethnicity, when we are instructed to appreciate diversity, but not to talk about race. It is about the new comparisons that teachers are able to make among minorities now that we are interested in what makes each ethnic group unique. In short, it is about the trade-offs that come with moving from social justice to diversity as the dominant frame for thinking about minority status.

Specifically, this book examines the unintended consequences of using diversity as the frame for understanding racial and ethnic difference within schools in the United States. I use the word *race* to mean the different resources and

1

recognition groups receive based on the perception of their phenotype. Ethnic- ity refers to the perceived cultural inheritance that a group has based on shared ancestry (Omi & Winant, 1994). The book argues that diversity talk pits ethnicity against race in U.S. schools. With its emphasis on the contributions of different races to society, the frame of diversity seems to be an improvement from the overt racism of the past which constructed minorities as inferior to Whites. However, the book shows that teachers use the discourse of diversity to create new hierar- chies among minority groups.

For the teachers portrayed in this book, diversity became a lens that magni- fied distinctions among minorities that have historically been treated as an undif- ferentiated mass. The lens altered the typical relationship between binaries such as foreign/native and familiar/strange (Kim, 1999). Teachers viewed native-born African Americans as familiar, yet alien in their values and experiences, but treat- ed Asian-American and Latino immigrants as foreign, but similar to themselves. This practice, termed racial triangulation, puts a new twist on racial/ethnic hierar- chies but does not eliminate them. The poles of the racial hierarchy remain Whites on top and Blacks on the bottom, but immigrant minorities come into focus as a separate group in the middle (Kim, 1999).

When teachers approached diversity this way, as a zero-sum game between minority groups, it had real costs for students and schools. Based on the logic of privileging ethnicity over race, teachers granted immigrant minorities such as Asians and Latinos advantages (*ethnic credits*) that Blacks did not receive. How- ever, I also show that Black students and schools suffer *racial penalties*, including stigma and its consequences, for being the wrong kind of different. Teachers' talk about diversity accomplished the impressive feat of seeming to move race rela- tions forward while actually holding old racial hierarchies in place and creating new ones.

Under this view, the elevation of multiracial schools will not result in the valu- ing of Black schools. Remember, the White teacher at the multiracial school liked her school because of the "cultures represented" in the neighborhood. Teachers will always overlook Blacks if the value of diversity comes from having a foreign culture. Thus, it was framing diversity as an appreciation of unfamiliar cultures that made it possible to value a multiracial school, but not a Black one.

Though the scenes happened at different types of school on different sides of town, they shared a way of thinking about minority groups. Teachers' negative perceptions of Black schools were tied to their positive perceptions of multiracial schools, even when teachers did not directly make comparisons between schools. In other words, the associations that teachers made were revealing, but so was the logic underlying how teachers talked about minority groups across schools.

Black schools were doubly estranged from how teachers valued minority sta- tus. First, teachers disfavored Black schools as single-race schools within a system that valued diversity. Yet, as we will see, teachers also felt enriched from teaching at predominantly Latino schools though they also were not diverse. It was not just the fact of being a single-race school, but the type of minority status which explained how teachers reacted to Black schools. Teachers saw Latino schools and students through the lens of ethnic difference, which added value to their minority status. In contrast, Black schools faced what I term *concentrated stigma* (or *stigma*) that was compounded by the Blackness of the students, faculty, and neighborhood of their schools, and by the fact that Blackness was the wrong type of different in many teachers' eyes. This stigma helps explain how at a glance the Black teacher "knew she wouldn't like it" at a Black school.

AUTOBIOGRAPHY OF A NAME: THE PERILS OF COLOR BLIND THINKING

While reading the book, it might be tempting to ridicule the teachers' comments. How could they say such prejudiced things, what were *they* thinking? To get away from making teachers a "them," so different from unbiased "us," I'd like to give an autobiography of my full name. The name Antonia Maria Randolph can take people by surprise, the Spanish-sounding first and middle names clashing with the Anglo-Saxon last name, and raise questions about my race and ethnicity. My names are uncommon for a Black woman in a country where being racially Black still means being ethnically African American to many. When I tell people that my mother is Costa Rican, my name makes more sense. In fact, they often become more interested in my background than they were before.

This book is about the forces that make us more curious about certain heritages than others and the consequences of making these distinctions. If the story of my name piqued your interest, made me seem more interesting, you likely responded out of the same multiculturalism that teachers do. Most of us are guilty of finding the "exotic" interesting—the teachers are not unique in this. However, the book will show our path to this curiosity is not innocent, but often motivated by a desire to avoid talking about race, injustice, and inequality. Moreover, a reason to express this curiosity is that it puts us in a good light—aren't we tolerant, aren't we knowledgeable and cosmopolitan? In that sense, the curiosity is instrumental, we want to know more because it benefits us, not just so we can connect with another person.

Finally, the curiosity about my name flattens my background. I am actually named after Lady Antonia Fraser, a British writer whom my mother admired. Thus, my first name owes as much to my mother's Anglophilia, born from the Jamaican origins of her family, as to her Costa Rican pride. This complicated heritage is necessarily flattened by those who apprehend my name, just as teachers flatten Latin-American and Asian-American students into perpetual immigrants no matter whether they are second- or third-generation Americans. In other words, I examine teachers' representations of race and ethnicity, not the reality of how students would identify themselves.

I write this book from two social locations, as–a Black woman and as a second generation Afro-Latina immigrant. The book grows out of the insight that my Afro-Latina heritage frequently makes me more interesting to strangers than my African-American heritage does. I view African American as an ethnicity, which is grounded in ancestry and national origin, but many people use the label interchangeably with Black, which I view as a race, or a reference to phenotype. Without knowing my background, I am simply African-American (read: Black), with a racial difference that seems impolite or even dangerous to ask about. But once a stranger finds out that I am also Afro-Latina (read: ethnic) through questions about my name, my background becomes a source of curiosity and pleasure. My difference becomes something that can be acknowledged and discussed; we can talk about it without either of us feeling uncomfortable. Thus, the ethnic nature of my difference as Afro-Latina allows my minority status to enter into discourse and renders it into a legitimate topic of discussion. Nevertheless, I use Black to refer to the racial and ethnic group in the rest of the book to make my terminology less confusing.

ORGANIZATION OF THE BOOK

The Wrong Kind of Different is based on one year of interviews with elementary school teachers at 11 schools in a large and diverse, yet segregated Midwestern city that I call Laketown. I was a member of the research team that conducted the interviews at schools as part of a larger study. We learned about the joys and frustrations of the teachers by observing them in classrooms, meetings, and break rooms, and interviewing them before and after their classes. I was the lead ethnographer at only one school, but I came to know the other schools through reading interviews conducted by other team members. Through these interviews I gained a deeper understanding of how teachers made sense of their everyday encounters with minority students.

This book is divided into six chapters. Chapter 1 gives a short history of major shifts in ideologies for responding to racial and ethnic diversity in schools, culminating in the racial orthodoxy of today. It argues that over time school racial policy has become unmoored from social justice, resulting in a practice that I term *assimilating diversity*. I identify the three main characteristics of assimilating diversity: (1) an ethnic paradigm of race that delegitimizes race and privileges ethnicity, (2) framing difference in terms of how it benefits the majority, and (3) preserving White normativity. The chapter ends by explaining the significance of assimilating diversity for creating new hierarchies among minority students and schools.

In Chapter 2, I show that teachers respond differently to the same problem, lack of parental involvement, depending on the race and ethnicity of students.

Teachers *credit* Latino parents for having good intentions based on an ethnic narrative of the well-meaning but ineffectual immigrant parent, and *penalize* Black parents for having bad intentions using the racial narrative of Black family dysfunction.

The next two chapters examine how student demographics affect the recruitment, retention, and job satisfaction of teachers. Chapter 3 examines teacher perceptions of multiracial schools, building on research which shows that White teachers tend to avoid schools with minority students and are less satisfied at those schools (Frankenberg, 2006). In contrast, teachers at the two multiracial schools that I studied wanted to teach at diverse schools because they felt enriched by having contact with other cultures. Teachers took an instrumental view of diversity and were drawn to the multicultural capital they gained from teaching at multiracial schools (Reay et al., 2007). However, they made distinctions between which minority groups add good and bad diversity to their schools.

Teachers at Black schools responded very differently than ones at multiracial schools. Chapter 4 shows that, instead of feeling lucky, teachers at Black schools felt stigmatized by the student population they served. "Black" or "inner-city" schools described more than student demographics; they symbolized schools that were underachieving, under resourced, disorderly, and violent. Teachers managed the stigma of teaching at Black schools by aspiring to have their school be seen as average. However, they sometimes missed the unique strengths and achievements of their school as they struggled to convince themselves and others that their school was no worse than the rest.

Though teachers expressed appreciation for immigrant minorities and ethnic difference, native-born, middle-class Whites were still the normative students. Chapter 5 shows the limits of the benefits that came from being an immigrant minority at school. The first section examines the ambiguous status of recent White European immigrants in teacher perceptions. The second section describes teachers' discomfort with the parts of immigrant minority culture that could not be consumed as funky exotica. The crux of this chapter is that middle-class native-born Whites remain the standard of value in the schools, preserving White normativity.

Chapter 6 concludes the book by arguing against the practice of assimilating diversity as a way of making sense of minority status. While assimilating diversity has had some positive effects, such as making multiracial schools desirable to teachers, it ultimately harms all minorities by focusing on benefits to the dominant group instead of social justice for minorities.

This book is for anyone who cares about how teachers make sense of diversity in our increasingly complex society. It captures teachers in the middle of their daily work and asks them to reflect on their practices. The teachers that you meet express the good feelings that many of us have when we think about the diversity of our society (Bell & Hartmann, 2007). Yet, they also show the pitfalls that can happen when we detach our appreciation of difference from concerns about social justice.

CHAPTER 1

Dividing Up Difference

"It's a mini United Nations basically. I think it's extremely unique to the city and it amazes me how well, you know, people tend to get along with each other. And I think these children—and I keep trying to tell them—don't realize how fortunate that they are that they're, you know, experienc(ing) this now while they're growing up because I think it's going to help them, you know, become more tolerant and understanding and more educated because we learn about everybody's culture, you know, whereas, if we didn't have the different ethnic groups we wouldn't."

—A White teacher at Dodge (a multiracial school),
describing the benefits of teaching at a diverse school

When it comes to talking about race and ethnicity, elementary school teachers are like many of us, well-intentioned, but sometimes unsure. Indeed, with the shifting parameters of what constitutes proper racial talk, it is hard to know what to say. On one hand, we are supposed to be a post-racial or color blind society, yet at the same time we are told to notice difference by celebrating diversity. Teachers are in the middle of these changes, having to make sense of diversity in the midst of doing their main job of teaching.

Still, the teacher whose quote begins the chapter does not seem at all uncertain about what he thinks of diversity. He thinks it is good: good for him, his city, and his students. The teacher expresses a view of diversity that is becoming increasingly common in America's schools. He compares his racially and ethnically diverse school favorably to the "United Nations." Moreover, he believes the diversity of his school will benefit its students, helping them become "more tolerant and understanding" of the differences in our multicultural society. This is diversity as lagniappe, an unexpected bonus.

This belief that racial and ethnic diversity benefits schools is new and still contested. It represents an increasingly orthodox way to navigate the terrain of difference that avoids the overt racism of the past, but contains other dangers that are less obvious. Specifically, are all minority groups included in this vision of school as the United Nations, just who makes up this beneficial diversity? Now that mainstream talk about race has moved away from virulent antipathy toward difference, we have to listen for different things in how teachers talk about race. Most importantly, we have to listen for silences, what goes unnamed as well as named, and distinctions, the subtle comparisons teachers make between groups (Pollock, 2001).

This book is the story of how teachers make sense of diversity in the course of their everyday interactions at school. It examines their race talk, or talk that treats racial and ethnic differences as salient, often to the detriment of racial and ethnic minorities (Myers & Williamson, 2001). Teachers had not meant their comments to be representative of other teachers, much less of broader trends in society. Indeed, most of them would not have said their comments were political, though I treat them as such. By *political*, I mean that the teachers' comments were informed by power relations among racial and ethnic groups and indicative of ideologies and discourses that are hegemonic in society. Teachers' race talk was political in its effect of perpetuating inequality among minority students.

The main proposition of this book is that teachers assimilate, or adapt, the practice of embracing diversity to the purpose of preserving the racial status quo of White dominance. In the abstract, embracing diversity could mean celebrating the unique strengths and contributions of all racial and ethnic groups in society. Yet, in practice teachers use the discourse of diversity to justify distinctions they make *between* groups of racial and ethnic minorities.

Teachers construct some forms of difference as legitimate and beneficial and others as illegitimate and harmful. They treat difference that they construct within the frame of ethnicity, using tropes of immigration, cultural heritage, and ancestry, as more legitimate than difference that they construct within a racial frame, using tropes of disadvantage and insurmountable, unchanging, or essential difference. By emphasizing ethnicity and delegitimizing race, teachers deny the continuing significance of racial discrimination and inequality while also seeming tolerant of difference. Put another way, teachers assimilate diversity by hitching multiculturalism to color blindness, which is the ideology that holds race is no longer a source of disadvantage and that to notice race is to be racist (Bonilla-Silva, 2003).

The quote that begins this chapter reflects a racial orthodoxy, or a constellation of ideas, beliefs, narratives, and practices around race that guide norms and expectations within an organization (Berrey, 2011). By definition, racial orthodoxies are widely shared, though not dominant, so I was surprised to find a similar orthodoxy across the 11 schools I studied. Teachers had similar ways of framing minority status that resulted in what I call *assimilating diversity*. By assimilating diversity, I mean adopting practices that value certain types of diversity but ultimately reinforce White normativity and maintain racial hierarchies.

Several practices constituted assimilating diversity. Teachers saw minority status through an ethnic paradigm of race (Omi & Winant, 1994) that relied on the narrative of rehabilitative ethnicity, or the notion that immigrants' ability to overcome obstacles proves that America is democratic (Hsu, 1996; Pierre, 2004); evaluated difference according to an instrumental logic that emphasized how diversity benefited them; all the while perpetuating White normativity. In using these practices, teachers created distinctions among racial minorities that raised the status of Asian Americans and Latinos above that of Blacks in schools.

Moreover, teachers' comments suggested that they symbolically rewarded students of color differently based on their race and ethnicity. Symbolic rewards are behaviors and attitudes that create a favorable climate for students. Specifically, teachers focused more on academics, showed more forgiveness toward uninvolved parents, and focused more on students' assets than deficits in their talk about Asian and Latino students than about Black students. Additionally, teachers spoke of being drawn to multiracial schools because of their diversity, yet reported being wary of Black schools because of the stigma surrounding them. In these ways, teachers rewarded Latinos and Asians for their ethnic difference, but penalized Blacks for having the wrong type of difference, one that was racially marked.

The distinctions teachers made among minorities provide evidence of the emerging tri-racial hierarchy that has begun to replace the traditional White-Black hierarchy in American society (Bonilla-Silva, 2004). Historically, the White-Black hierarchy did not distinguish among minority groups, but rather rewarded Whites and penalized all racial and ethnic minority groups. However, new immigration policy has enabled racial minorities to arrive from Latin America, Asia, and the Caribbean who have more education and skills, and thus greater social mobility than native-born minorities such as Blacks and Native Americans (O'Connor, 2001). This greater variation in minority mobility has eroded the binary that fixed Whites in advantaged and minorities in disadvantaged social positions. The new system leaves native-born Whites at the top and Blacks at the bottom, but separates out Latinos and Asians in the middle of the status hierarchy (Bonilla-Silva, 2004).

Teachers attend to differences among minority groups in the face of this diversified minority population. Scholars have previously noted that certain groups of immigrant minorities, that is, those who are minorities due to migration, have higher achievement than native-born minorities, that is, those who are minorities due to conquest, genocide, and enslavement (Ogbu, 1995). Research has mainly cited the cultural differences between immigrant and native-born minorities to explain the higher achievement of immigrant minorities (Bankston, 2004; Ogbu, 1995). Yet, I show that teachers make distinctions between immigrant and native-born minorities that provide relative advantages to immigrant minorities. This suggests that the differences in minority achievement may also be due to disparities in teacher perceptions of those groups.

Teachers make comparisons that pit Asians and Latinos against Blacks in their race talk through a process called racial triangulation (Kim, 1999). Historically, the dominant culture constructed Blacks and Whites as polar opposites, believing that characteristics that one group had were completely absent in the other group. Now, the dominant culture establishes the status of minority groups not just by comparing them to itself, but comparing them to each other. A well-known version of this comparison is to contrast Asians as successful, model minorities with Blacks as a racial underclass (Kim, 1999). Modern race talk constructs minority groups as both similar to and different from the dominant group, not just as opposites.

Yet, the typical portrayal of Asians as model minorities only acknowledges the superior/inferior axis of the field of racial positioning. Racial triangulation theory shows that Asian Americans are also marked as perpetually foreign, which disadvantages them on the American/foreign scale (Kim, 1999). Asians (and Latinos) experience relative elevation of their status, but also ostracism due to never being fully embraced as citizens (Kim, 1999). Thus, racial triangulation theory contends that despite apparently granting status to some minority groups, modern racial dynamics act as a way of maintaining White supremacy (Kim, 1999).

Another cornerstone of the racial orthodoxy in the schools I studied, besides racial triangulation, was diversity discourse. Diversity discourse celebrates diversity while minimizing race's role as a system of power and disadvantage, and casts diversity in terms of its benefit to the dominant group (Berrey, 2011; Embrick, 2011). Diversity discourse can be race conscious, though often in a way that empties race of its social impact (Berrey, 2011), and is likely to convert race into redemptive cultural differences (Gallagher, 2003). While diversity discourse pushes teachers toward a murky kind of "happy talk" about difference (Bell & Hartmann, 2007), racial triangulation sharpens teachers' focus on distinctions between minority groups, separating the good diversity of immigrant minorities out from the bad diversity of native-born minorities, particularly African Americans.

The rest of this chapter reviews the history and consequences of the way teachers divide up difference. I argue that teachers have consistently rewarded groups they constructed as having an ethnic difference and overlooked or penalized groups they constructed as having a racial difference. I also explain the theoretical tools of this book, including a more detailed explanation of assimilating diversity. Finally, I explain how the location of the study affected the way teachers made sense of diversity.

FROM ASSIMILATION TO PLURALISM: A HISTORY OF RACE AND ETHNICITY IN EARLY 20TH-CENTURY AMERICAN SCHOOLS

Essentially, American attitudes toward minorities reflect our beliefs about whether social difference is desirable or undesirable. This dilemma can be characterized as the choice between erasing differences between social groups in order to preserve national unity, and, thus idealizing an un-hyphenated American identity, or preserving difference as a positive link to the past that does not threaten allegiance to American values and policy (Tyack, 2003). To put it another way, we can think about the dilemma about the desirability of diversity as a debate over whether particular minority groups are valuable to society thus, the nation has struggled over whether minorities detract from or enhance society because of their minority status.

Racial and ethnic minorities have historically had a troubled place in American schools. The United States has always had an ambivalent relationship to its status as a nation of immigrants, not to mention its legacy of forcibly incorporating Africans, Native Americans, and Mexicans into the country (Farley, 2005). The Founding Fathers put schools at the center of the debate over social diversity and saw the common public school as the mechanism for Americanizing newcomers and providing them with an opportunity for social mobility (Tyack, 2003). The common school system, which made free public school available to all children, not just the children of elites, was seen as a testament to the United States' commitment to democracy. Yet, the Founding Fathers made no provisions for securing the mobility of minorities that were already in their midst, such as Blacks and Native Americans, when establishing the common school.

From this beginning, two central themes can be seen in American schools' response to minorities: first, a faith that school can be a tool of social democracy, and second, a focus on the experience of White ethnic immigrants as the model for understanding how to address social diversity coupled with an inattention to the plight of native-born minorities. As we will see, these two tendencies color teacher perceptions of minorities today.

Historical Treatment of White Ethnic Immigrants

Historically, schools advanced different policies toward minority students depending on whether assimilation or pluralism was in favor. Initially, assimilation guided national policy toward racial and ethnic minorities. Between the 1890s and the 1920s American public schools tried to naturalize the new wave of Southern and Eastern European immigrants that were arriving by making school mandatory for all children and insisting that classes be taught in English (Tyack, 2003). Schools' interest in naturalizing immigrant students was not merely altruistic, but a response to the changing demographics of America's schools. According to one study, between 1908 and 1909 57.8% of all students in 37 American cities were children of immigrants, that is, second-generation immigrants (Fass, 1989, p. 42).

Though most educators thought assimilation should be the ultimate goal of the education of immigrants, by the 1920s and 1930s some progressive educators also believed that a measure of pluralism could ease the way to assimilation. For example, some educators thought that pluralistic practices, such as celebrating the special contributions of immigrant culture or encouraging second generation students to learn about their parents' culture, could make immigrants' transition to an American way of life less jarring (Tyack, 2003). Thus, during the 1920s and 1930s the assimilationist approach to immigrants was tempered by a pluralistic willingness to incorporate some aspects of immigrant culture into school. This willingness to accommodate differences suggested that schools saw some social value in what White European immigrants contributed to American society. By the end of the 1930s, American schools' success in incorporating these new European immigrants into the school system was heralded as a cardinal sign of America's progress toward social democracy (Fass, 1989).

However, the social value of White ethnic groups that emerged in the 1920s and 1930s, while greater than it was under strict assimilation, was nevertheless limited in a major regard. American schools' enthusiasm for the social difference of immigrants was tempered by their frustration with the difficulty of teaching immigrant students. Schools were faced with the need to educate increasing numbers of children who were diverse. This proved hard to do as immigrant student achievement lagged behind that of their native-born White counterparts. For instance, at that time in New York 40.4% of second-generation American students were 2 years behind the grade level they should have been according to their age (Fass, 1989, p. 42). Thus, under the pluralism of the 1930s, schools perceived immigrant students as socially valuable as long as their presence did not interfere with another emerging social value, efficient teaching (Fass, 1989). Schools' evaluation of minority students' social value was counterbalanced by whether they perceived students as detracting from the schools' progress, a point to which I will return in Chapter 3.

To address the dual pressures of incorporating more immigrants while teaching more efficiently, American schools developed the practice of targeting curriculum to the individual differences of students (Fass, 1989). An important aspect of the targeted curriculum was its assumption that differences in achievement between social groups were natural and unchangeable (Fass, 1989). Based on the racial pseudoscience of the day, schools began to view White European immigrants' achievement disparity with native-born Whites using a "racial" lens. This belief in the insurmountable nature of group differences allowed American schools to claim to hold fast to their commitment to teaching all Americans, that is, their commitment to pluralism, yet immigrant and native-born Whites were educated differently (Fass, 1989).

The previous discussion suggests that concepts of race and ethnicity were always at play in American schools' response to social diversity. The European ethnic groups that were filling public schools in the 1920s and 1930s would now be considered White, yet during that earlier time period many of them would have been considered racially other (Tyack, 2003). For instance, social historians have shown that the Irish, Jews, and Italians were considered racially different from native-born American Whites at this time (Guglielmo, 2003; Jacobson, 1999). This racial difference was on the minds of educators as they constructed their policies toward Southern and Eastern European immigrants. For example, some educators believed that the racial inferiority of Southern European immigrants placed them beyond the help of education and felt the best policy was to reduce immigration to the United States (Tyack, 2003). Eventually, American society came to perceive these groups as Whites, but this shift in racial status was not guaranteed at the time. Nevertheless, the eventual assimilation of European immigrants shaped schools' response to involuntary minorities and to subsequent waves of immigrants.

Historical Treatment of Blacks

Even as schools accommodated the diversity introduced by European immigrants, they were slow to respond to the diversity posed by native-born minorities. Here, the other tendency of American policy toward minorities, the one where schools overlook the conditions of native-born minorities, comes to the forefront. Clearly, native-born minorities such as Mexican Americans and Native Americans had been part of the national populace long before the arrival of the new wave of European immigrants at the turn of the 20th century. Yet, American schools chose to construct the problem of social diversity in schools as a matter of incorporating White European immigrants, not native-born minorities, into school (Fass, 1989). For instance, American public schools did not pay attention to the under-education of African Americans until the 1930s and 1940s, and only then because the Great Depression and World War II made the illiteracy of potential Black soldiers and workers a national concern (Fass, 1989). However, once Black education became part of the national consciousness, the education of minorities became a matter of federal policy and has remained so ever since (Fass, 1989).

America's belated attention to the education of Blacks and other native-born minorities is a sign of the extent to which these groups were considered outside of mainstream society (Fass, 1989). Further, their racial difference was what made these groups beyond the scope of the pluralistic concern for inclusion. While America was lauding itself for incorporating White European immigrants into its schools, they were simultaneously ignoring the even more dire under-education of minorities that were already in residence. As poorly as White European immigrants had it, involuntary minorities had it worse. During the 1930s and 1940s the Black population in America, which was predominantly Southern, faced segregated and unequal schools in addition to a paucity of high schools to serve them (Fass, 1989). Thus, America's push toward social democracy through education met its limit when it encountered the racial difference of native-born minorities.

When the spotlight focused on native-born minorities, the American school system began to compare their achievement with that of immigrants. By the time the educational system began to respond to the needs of Blacks in the 1940s, White European immigrants had already started to increase their achievement and blend in with the native-born White population. Today the assimilation is complete and there is no achievement gap between native-born Whites and the children of Eastern and Southern European immigrants. However, a gap has emerged between the achievement of Whites and native-born minorities and between native-born and immigrant minorities (Ogbu, 1995). This achievement gap has again raised concerns about America's ability to incorporate all minorities into society through education.

RACING PERCEPTIONS:
DISPARATE TEACHER PERCEPTIONS OF MINORITY STUDENTS

Since the 1990s, most studies of teacher perceptions find that teachers have negative perceptions of Black and Latino students and positive perceptions of Asian and White students. For example, a representative overview of the research shows that teachers feel greater social distance from Black students, would choose to eliminate them from their classes if they could, and have low expectations of their achievement and educational attainment (Ferguson, 1998). Other research shows that teachers have equally negative perceptions of Blacks and Latinos but positive perceptions of Whites (Ehrenberg & Brewer, 1995).

In contrast, teachers are likely to have positive perceptions of Asian students, particularly, by attributing to them good values. Thus, a study found that teachers were more likely to perceive Asian, rather than Black or Latino students, as "good school citizens," defined as exhibiting pro-school behavior and following the rules and norms of school (Farkas, Sheehan, Grobe, & Shuan, 1990). Another study found that teachers preferred teaching the "well-behaved and hardworking" "immigrant students," code words for Asians, whom they implicitly contrasted with "lazy" Black and Latino students (Rosenbloom & Way, 2004). The authors noted that teachers deliberately used racial code words such as "immigrant students" to avoid being accused of being racist for the distinctions they made.

Similarly, research in Australia and England found that teachers attribute Asian students with an "ethnic success ethic," defined as having respect for elders, motivation to succeed, and supportive parents that derived from Asian cultural values (Archer & Francis, 2005; Bullivant, 1988). Likewise, an Irish study found that teachers have more positive perceptions of African, Southeast Asian, and Chinese students than of working-class White students due to the pro-school values they attribute to immigrant minorities (Devine, 2005). This suggests that immigrant minorities can sometimes outrank native-born Whites in teacher perceptions, in certain circumstances.

Moreover, teachers have tended to perceive minority school composition as detracting from rather than increasing the quality and desirability of schools. Pre-service teachers express an aversion to minority or multiracial school composition. For instance, research revealed that White pre-service teachers had little experience with or knowledge of students of color and felt unprepared to teach them as a result (Sleeter, 2000). This discomfort was borne out in a survey which found that White college students in a teacher training program had more interest in teaching at private and suburban schools than at Black or Latino urban schools (Groulx, 2001). White teacher perceptions are crucial since research shows that 83% of public school teachers are White yet 42% of public school students are people of color (Frankenberg, 2006).

Thus, both nationally and internationally, research shows that teachers have negative perceptions of the achievement and values of certain minorities, but not others. Historically, the literature focused on teacher perceptions of Black students, which tended to be negative. However, as immigrant minorities increase as a proportion of the minority population, it is important to understand the distinctions teachers make among minority groups. Research thus far shows that teachers racially triangulate Asian students in the United States and various immigrant minority groups in Europe above the status of native-born minorities.

CONSEQUENCES OF DISPARITIES IN TEACHER PERCEPTIONS OF MINORITY STUDENTS

Research has shown that the racial disparity in teacher perceptions of students helps sustain the achievement gap between races. Much of this literature focuses on the way teacher perceptions affect Black achievement, though there are some studies on Latino and Asian students. On the whole, teacher perceptions seem to negatively affect Black and Latino student achievement and positively affect Asian achievement. While this book focuses on teacher perceptions, it is nonetheless important to sketch the disparate consequences of these perceptions for students of color.

Effect on Students: Self-Fulfilling Prophecy and School Climate

Teacher perceptions affect student outcomes through self-fulfilling effects, differential teacher practice, differential school climate, and impaired recruitment and retention of good teachers at minority schools. Teacher negative perceptions have adversely affected Black students by creating a self-fulfilling prophecy in which students lower their achievement in response to the low expectations teachers have of them (Rist, 1970). Scholars also have speculated that teachers' positive perceptions of Asian students have a self-fulfilling effect on their high achievement; however, more research needs to be done in this area (Bankston, 2004).

Teacher perceptions can also affect teachers' instructional practice in ways that can impact student achievement. Studies have found that teachers create a warmer classroom climate, give more difficult material, more helpful feedback, and wait longer for responses from White students than Black students (Casteel, 1998). Moreover, a meta-analysis found that Black and Latino students' interactions with their teachers were more negative and fewer in number than those of White students, possibly as a result of differences in teacher perceptions by students' race (Cooper & Allen, 1998). In addition, some teachers with negative perceptions of minorities lower their standards and even abdicate their responsibility for teaching minority students (Diamond & Spillane, 2004).

Effect on Teachers: Recruitment and Retention

Teacher perceptions could also affect the recruitment and retention of good teachers to schools with high minority populations. Teachers with negative perceptions of minority students might be less likely to want to teach at minority schools and less likely to stay at those schools once on staff. This is an important potential outcome, since research shows that minority schools have more trouble attracting highly credentialed teachers than White schools (Ferguson, 1998).

While few studies have examined this proposition directly, related research suggests that teacher perceptions might affect teacher retention. For instance, a study (Alexander, Entwisle, & Thompson, 1987) found that teachers feel less satisfaction when they teach at minority schools; similarly, another study (Freeman, Brookhart, & Loadman, 1999) found that new teachers feel less satisfied at minority schools than those at mostly White schools. Likewise, other research finds that White teachers had lower job satisfaction and school commitment at minority schools than Black teachers at White schools (Mueller & Price, 1999). If the teachers who feel dissatisfied are also good teachers, they may be harder to keep at minority schools.

FROM PLURALISM TO ASSIMILATING DIVERSITY: THEORIZING LAKETOWN'S RACIAL ORTHODOXY

Based on the preceding discussion of the research there are some clear trends in how race and ethnicity have affected teacher perception of students. During the early 20th century, American schools moved from a policy of assimilating minority students and erasing difference to a practice of limited pluralism. This switch in practice was due to demographic changes (i.e., the influx of Southern and Eastern European immigrants) as well as a change in the dominant ideology of incorporation from absolute assimilation to an accommodation of difference. Still, schools practiced pluralism for assimilationist ends, since they hoped pluralism would hasten European immigrants' integration into American society. Schools believed that once immigrant students satisfied their curiosity by learning about their homelands, they could settle into becoming full Americans.

Nevertheless, the pluralism of acknowledging White immigrants' ethnic heritage in schools of the past is very different than the multiculturalism of today. Thus, the second major shift in America's racial orthodoxy was from pluralism to multiculturalism as the guiding ideology. In the 1920s and 1930s, schools thought that teaching European immigrants about their heritage would only benefit the immigrants themselves (Tyack, 2003). In contrast, modern multiculturalism holds that learning about the ethnic heritage of diverse groups benefits the entire school, not just the minority group (Berrey, 2011).

Moreover, European immigrants were the only candidates for pluralism and ultimately integration into American society because they were considered White; American schools were less accommodating of the diversity posed by native-born minorities. While Eastern and Southern Europeans did not start off as White in the American imagination, they became White over time. Schools did not offer native-born minorities such as African Americans the same chance to have their difference acknowledged in school until the civil rights struggles of the 1960s resulted in the establishment of multiculturalism in the 1980s (McCarthy, 1993). Yet, the multiculturalism that became dominant in schools was color blind and erased or downplayed racial inequality and concentrated on respect for cultural differences such as language, food, and customs (Ladson-Billings, 1996). Color blind multiculturalism has made American schools color conscious, but race blind.

Components of Assimilating Diversity

Assimilating diversity has three components: ethnicizing minority status; practicing productive diversity, or emphasizing how diversity benefits the dominant group; and reproducing White normativity.

Ethnicizing Minority Status. The assertion that race and ethnicity matter to teachers is not new. However, this book differs from other works by examining how teachers deploy racial and ethnic discourse to achieve particular ends. I treat racial and ethnic discourse as instruments of power. Ethnic discourse is not inherently conservative, that is, preserving of the status quo, but the dominant group has used ethnicity, in combination with ideologies such as meritocracy, to normalize and legitimate racial inequality (Hsu, 1996). Ethnic discourse, which converts structural differences between groups into differences between cultural heritages, became more important as racial minorities became more diverse. It allowed Whites to point to the success of "model minorities" such as Asians to argue that cultural differences, not structural barriers due to race, explain Black underachievement. This book provides an empirical study of how this "rehabilitative concept of ethnicity" is mobilized in the school context (Hsu, 1996). Thus, the distinction between race and ethnicity is the linchpin to my argument about how minority status operates in schools.

Productive Diversity. Teachers practice *productive diversity* by thinking about difference in terms of how it enriches schools (The New London Group, 1996). In other words, they have an instrumental, rather than a social justice, view of diversity (Reay et al., 2007). The logic of productive diversity has made its way into higher education, as evidenced by the orthodoxy of defending Affirmative Action as a means to enrich institutions due to diversity rather than as a means for rectifying inequality (Berrey, 2011). This book is among the first to document how the logic of productive diversity has trickled down into primary schools.

The hierarchies teachers create between minority groups are informed by the current value placed on that group's difference. Teachers seek to acquire *multicultural capital*, the prestige that comes from knowing about valued foreign cultures and from having contact with foreign groups (Reay et al., 2007). Throughout this book, I offer teachers' responses to African Americans to show the underside of this valuation process. Black difference is rendered valueless in the symbolic economy described here. Teachers did not perceive Blacks as having an ethnicity, understood as having a distinct cultural heritage that results from immigrant ancestry, nor did they perceive race as a legitimate or enriching source of difference. The twin forces of multiculturalism and color blindness placed African Americans outside the market of symbolic value.

Perpetuating White Normativity. A theme of this book is that teachers value and reward immigrant minorities such as Latinos and Asians for how they enrich their schools. The value teachers place on particular minority groups does not displace White normativity, however. Indeed, scholars have pointed out the "racial unconscious" of multiculturalism that affirms Whiteness as the standard by which other racial and ethnic groups should be measured even while celebrating difference (Jung, 2009). As this book will show, teachers recognized differences that complement America's self-perception as an open and inclusive society that has fashioned racial harmony out of diversity. Teachers are less accepting of differences that do not fulfill this ideological role, differences that are not enriching, but are merely "other," or are threatening in some way. Thus, teachers' celebration of diversity happened within the context of reaffirming the normativity of Whiteness.

LAKETOWN: DIVERSITY EAST COAST STYLE

We cannot understand the way teachers made sense of difference and the manner in which they assimilated diversity without considering Laketown as a context. Laketown is a large, diverse, Midwestern city that could be any big city on the east coast of the United States. Like many Eastern cities, Laketown was an economic powerhouse that was trying to find its footing in the post-industrial era. Laketown survived the switch to a service economy somewhat better than some of its neighbors, but its prosperity was not evenly distributed among racial and ethnic groups. Thus, though government and businesses were investing in Laketown by gentrifying certain neighborhoods, this development did nothing to alleviate the concentrated poverty caused by hyper-segregation in other parts of town. Laketown shared this pattern of unequal development with many other Midwestern and Northern cities of the late 1990s.

Like many Eastern cities, Laketown was racially diverse, yet also very segregated. While we can find cities across America that contain many races and ethnicities who nonetheless live separately, the complexion of Laketown's diversity is typical of the Midwest and the Northeast. For one thing, Laketown's Black population was predominantly African American, not of immigrant heritage. This meant teachers expected Black students to be native-born. The assumption that Black means African American is common in most major Eastern cities, except for New York (and perhaps New Jersey), where teachers have more awareness of Black ethnic diversity (Warikoo, 2004).

In addition, while Laketown was a multiracial city, the Black-White racial split shaped teachers' racial imagination. Though the city had large Latino and Asian populations, its public discourse often focused on relations between Blacks and Whites. This focus on Black-White racial dynamics is still typical of the east coast, but not of the west coast, where Latinos and Asians loom larger in the public racial imagination. Finally, Laketown had a history of White ethnic enclaves that was common to Eastern cities. However, it also had a sizeable population of recent immigrants from Eastern Europe that was distinctive. When teachers talked about White students, they were also aware of a portion of Whites that were not native-born, but were recent immigrants.

Laketown was diverse, but it was diversity east coast style. It was a city fighting to regain its former glory rather than a Western or Sunbelt boom city. It was a multiracial, multiethnic city that was haunted by the specter of Black-White relations. It was a city that recognized ethnic diversity among Whites, but not among Blacks. These features made the racial meaning-making in Laketown typical of a certain type of big American city, one that was on the east coast.

The combination of racial and ethnic groups that constituted Laketown's population shaped teacher perceptions of diversity. The ongoing salience of the Black-White racial divide affected teacher perceptions of other racial/ethnic minorities. This was especially true of the way teachers' racially triangulated students. Though Laketown contained several different racial and ethnic minority groups, teachers seemed to judge minorities against Blacks. As racial triangulation theory predicts, teachers positioned Blacks on the inferior end of the inferior-superior scale of status and located other minority groups within the middle of that scale (Kim, 1999). Teachers associated Black students and schools, but not other racial and ethnic minorities, with lack.

This book analyzes interviews with teachers at 11 public elementary schools that represented the dominant school compositions in the city. Thus, the sample included seven predominantly Black schools, two predominantly Latino schools,

Table 1.1. Student Demographics

School Demographics	BLACK SCHOOLS							LATINO SCHOOLS		MULTIRACIAL SCHOOLS	
	Brantley	Erving	Foster	Kipps	Martin	Noel	Watts	Putnam	Stanley	Bowen	Dodge
Grade Levels	K–8	K–8	K–8	preK–8	preK–8	preK–8	preK–8	preK–6	preK–8	preK–8	K–8
Enrollment	830	215	618	302	1046	1035	356	939	1363	1118	1507
% Low Income	98.7	70.2	99.4	88.4	95.4	97.6	92.4	96.3	95.3	64.0	71.6
% Black	100.0	99.5	100.0	100.0	99.7	99.5	100.0	2.8	4.3	6.1	8.2
% White	0.0	0.0	0.0	0.0	0.3	0.0	0.0	0.5	3.6	44.5	39.2
% Latino	0.0	0.5	0.0	0.0	0.0	0.5	0.0	96.4	92.0	25.3	21.6
% Asian	0.0	0.0	0.0	0.0	0.0	0.0	0.0	0.3	0.1	23.4	30.9

Table 1.2. Teacher Demographics

School	Black	White	Latino	Asian	Total
Bowen	3	9	0	1	13
Brantley	5	1	0	0	6
Dodge	3	18	1	3	25
Erving	1	1	0	0	2
Foster	2	1	0	0	3
Kipps	5	2	0	0	7
Martin	9	2	0	0	11
Noel	4	1	0	0	5
Putnam	0	3	3	0	6
Stanley	2	10	4	0	16
Watts	4	2	0	0	6
Total	38	50	8	4	100

and two multiracial schools. At predominantly Black and Latino schools, the respective racial/ethnic group made up more than 90% of the student population. In contrast, multiracial schools had significant percentages of at least three or more racial/ethnic groups (see Table 1.1). Table 1.2 shows the racial composition of teachers in the sample. The table shows that Whites were the predominant racial group in the sample, which is typical of American school teachers (Frankenberg, 2006).

The upcoming chapters present the underside of multiculturalism and diversity discourse. They show the perils of racial triangulation. On one hand, we could have never predicted from America's assimilationist past that a White teacher would one day come to laud the diversity at his school, as the teacher does at the beginning of this chapter. Yet, while assimilating diversity appears to be a step toward a more democratic and just society, it may have the exact opposite effect. The following chapters show teachers cementing the distinctions among minority groups, while using language that celebrates diversity and honors difference. Thus, our new infatuation with diversity may wind up reinforcing old racial hierarchies and creating new ones if we do not pay closer attention to what teachers are and are not saying.

CHAPTER 2

"I Admire Hispanic People"
Ethnic Credits and Racial Penalties in the Classroom

The negative perceptions teachers have of minority students are a perennial concern for educational research. Yet, the increasing diversity within the minority student population warrants a new look at teacher perceptions. The quote that provides the title for this chapter illustrates this point. It comes from a Black teacher at a mostly Latino elementary school who described her school as being located in "a working class neighborhood" in the "inner city."

Based on previous research, we might expect the teacher to have negative perceptions of her students due to their low status and racial mismatch, or the racial difference between her students and herself (Alexander et al., 1987). Contrary to expectations, the teacher comments that the neighborhood is a "thriving community" even though "there is a lot of poverty." She went on to say, "I admire Hispanic people because they might not have a dime but their children are taken care of. Their clothes are clean. They try to provide what they can for their children." In her estimation, Latino students have decency, due to their Latino heritage, which belies their poverty.

This quote touches on the issues of minority status, morality, and symbolic value that animate this chapter. Across schools teachers ascribed good morals to minorities, such as Latinos and Asians, whom they constructed using the ethnic discourse of cultural inheritance derived from national origin. However, this type of admiration was absent in teachers' talk about Black students, whom they often cast as needing rescue from their morally bankrupt families and communities. Not incidentally, teachers constructed Black students using a racial discourse that treated Blackness as insurmountably different from mainstream society.

This chapter examines the credits and penalties that come from racial and ethnic distinctions teachers make between students. The type of narrative, either racial or ethnic, teachers used to construct students greatly influenced their perceptions of students of color. Teachers constructed Black students using the racialized narrative of the culture of poverty, which blamed student disadvantages on their lack of mainstream values (Pierre, 2004). In contrast, teachers constructed Asian and Latino students using what I call the "decent immigrant" narrative, which lauds them for maintaining their morality in the face of debasing circumstances.

The discrepancy in response to minorities is due to the "symbolic currency," or value to the dominant discourse about American society, that is attached to ethnic (as opposed to racial) narratives of minority status (Hsu, 1996; Pierre, 2004). Ethnic narratives, which are based on the experience of White immigrants during the early 20th century, say that minority status is an impermanent obstacle that can be overcome through hard work and the proper values (Gallagher, 2003; Hsu, 1996). Teachers reward ethnicized minority students with benefits such as positive perceptions and high expectations, when they succeed or display mainstream values.

At the same time, teachers punish minority students that they construct using racial narratives with penalties such as negative perceptions, low expectations, and denial of other symbolic resources. Under this view, race is tainted with associations of lasting disadvantage and deviant values that put America's democratic self-image in a bad light (Pierre, 2004). While students have both racial identities (such as Black or White) and ethnic identities (such as Mexican or Korean), teachers were more likely to ethnicize Asians and Latinos and racialize Black students. Thus, teachers constructed a symbolic field of value in which Asian and Latino students received what I call "ethnic credits" for their minority status, while Black students received "racial penalties."

This chapter deals with the first component of assimilating diversity, ethnicizing minority status. Attributing immigrant minorities with morality is just one way to pit immigrant minorities against native-born minorities. One could also construct a story that says immigrant minorities are more grateful for their opportunities, as migrants in search of a better life, than native-born minorities and thus work harder in school. Indeed, we could create any number of stories that tell why immigrant status gives immigrant minorities virtues that native-born minorities do not have. Thus, the specific stories that teachers tell about immigrant and native-born minorities are not as important as the fact that they reward minorities that fit within an ethnic narrative, one which says the thing that makes you different will ultimately make you successful. When teachers ethnicize minority status in this way, they throw Blacks into relief as outliers.

THE STORY OF DIFFERENCE:
RACE AND ETHNICITY AS NARRATIVES

Race is a story that we tell about human difference. On its surface, race is a story that takes physical differences and ascribes them with social meaning (Omi & Winant, 1994). However, race does not just offer the categories, Black, White, Asian, and Native American, in which to place groups of people; it provides a narrative which tells us how to feel about them. Most scholars go beyond this surface understanding of race and think of it as a system of power that unequally distributes resources among groups of people. Yet, race does not just specify social locations within a hierarchy of power; it describes the sort of individuals who live there.

Ethnicity is also a story, one which overlaps with race, but is not subsumed by it. Where the story of race extrapolates from physical differences, the story of ethnicity is fashioned from national origin and shared cultural inheritance. The United States divides the same cast of characters up differently when using the narrative of ethnicity instead of race, for instance, by substituting Korean American or African American to describe individuals that race would label as Asian or Black.

A key step toward assimilating diversity, or acknowledging difference in a way that maintains racial hierarchies, is to only value ethnic difference. The narratives described below reward students when their difference can be understood using an ethnic frame. They see the values of mainstream society in the stories they tell about immigrant minorities.

DESERVING AND UNDESERVING MINORITIES: TEACHERS' ETHNIC AND RACIAL NARRATIVES

Teachers used three ethnic narratives and three racial narratives to describe students. The ethnic narratives were the ethnic culture of poverty, immigrant status as a burden, and the decent immigrant. The racial narratives were the at-risk student, the culture of poverty, and social responsibility. I was especially interested in the narratives teachers used to construct Blacks and Latinos, since they ascribed poverty and lack of parental involvement to both groups.

Most narratives, both ethnic and racial, were associated with negative teacher perceptions (see Table 2.1). Still, teachers had positive perceptions of Whites, Latinos, and Asians when using the decent immigrant narrative and positive perceptions of Blacks when using the social responsibility narrative. However, Black teachers were nearly the only ones to use the social responsibility narrative, which limited Black students' chances for receiving positive perceptions. Moreover, teachers had a more optimistic view of immigrant minorities, even when they focused on their deficits. In this way, teachers credited immigrant minorities for their ethnic difference while they penalized African Americans for their racial difference.

Ethnic Narratives

Ethnic Culture of Poverty. Three main themes constitute this narrative: poverty, danger, and morality. Teachers overwhelmingly used this narrative to discuss Latinos, rather than Asians or Whites. I distinguish the ethnic culture of poverty from the traditional culture of poverty narrative for several reasons. One difference

Table 2.1. Ethnic and Racial Narratives by Teacher Perceptions

Ethnic Narratives	Positive Perceptions	Negative Perceptions
Ethnic culture of poverty	6	7
Immigrant status as burden	11	19
Decent immigrant	17	8
Racial narratives		
Culture of poverty	9	20
At-risk kids	2	11
Social responsibility	7	4

Numbers represent number of interviews.
Racial narratives only refer to Blacks; ethnic narratives refer to Whites, Latinos, and Asians.

is that teachers used poverty as a descriptive, not moral, category when talking about Latinos. Also, teachers associated violence with the neighborhood, not with the kids. They say the neighborhoods are dangerous because they are poor, not because the kids are violence-prone. Ultimately, this narrative tells a story of minorities who refuse to be demoralized by a demoralizing environment.

An example from a Latina teacher at a Latino school was typical. She described her students' material deprivation while attesting to their decency. She said, "The parents that I meet on the street are very cordial. I would say that it may be a poor neighborhood, but it's a safe neighborhood for the most part." She believed the decency of the parents, the fact they were "cordial," minimized the risk for violence in the community. Earlier, when asked how she would characterize the neighborhood, she said:

> It's a safe neighborhood. There may be random acts of gang violence, whatever, but for the length of time that I have been working here, I don't drive. I take (public transportation) from downtown into the neighborhood and I take (it) out of the neighborhood. I have never had an incident, never ever, ever and I travel at strange hours. I get to school at seven in the morning.

The teacher was willing to bet her personal safety on her perception that the neighborhood violence was "isolated." This portrait of the neighborhood had the elements of the culture of poverty story, with neighborhood disorganization represented by gang violence and poverty, but the disorder did not harden the hearts of its residents.

Indeed, a White teacher at the other Latino school even saw decency in gang members. Like the previous teacher, she said she was "not afraid to come to school." She continued:

I know there are kids that are in gangs, but even those kids are not disrespectful. I think it's a great place to be. . . . I like coming here every day and it's a good place to teach. The parents are great. Kids are good by and large. You know, you always have the yo-yos.

The respectability of the parents seems crucial to her perception of the neighborhood. Earlier in the interview she said she found the parents "cooperative" and felt able to "get things done" with them. Her good feeling toward the parents turned into optimism toward the kids. Her kids had "great" parents who taught them not to be "disrespectful" even if they were in gangs.

Her faith in Latino decency allowed her to enjoy teaching at the school despite the potentially dangerous students in her class. She made violence seem unlikely by conceding that "you always have the yo-yos," but insisting that the students were well-behaved "by and large." Teachers used qualifiers such as "by and large," "random," and "isolated" throughout the narrative to mark violence as contrary to the basic decency of Latinos. In short, teachers credited Latino students with morality that muted the negativity of their perceptions of them.

Teachers focused on within-school solutions to the ethnic culture of poverty, for instance, by teaching students to be leaders so they would not want to join gangs or by giving students time during the school day to talk about violence they may have experienced. Their response was empathetic, but meant only to quell problems at school. For instance, the Latina assistant principal at a Latino school started a mediation program at her school to create a sense of "safety for all our children—the good ones and the naughty ones." Teachers had an individual rather than a structural response to the ethnic culture of poverty.

Immigrant Status as Burden. This narrative featured stories about how aspects of immigrant status, especially having a language barrier, hampered student achievement. Yet, teachers did not treat the language barrier as a moral failing, but instead constructed it as a legitimate deficit. A Black teacher at a Latino school saw a direct connection between the language barrier and academic achievement. In response to a question about students' strengths and weaknesses, she said:

I think it's wonderful to be bilingual but it's also we live in the United States of America and English is the official language. And I think one huge weakness is many of our students do not speak Standard English. And it cripples them when we have these standardized tests. . . . And it's because, first of all, second language acquisition is so difficult, it takes a long time. Not just a couple years, but it takes a very long time. Secondly, Standard English is not spoken at home. . . . That in my mind, that's a weakness.

The teacher was careful to note that she "thinks it's wonderful to be bilingual," which befit the norm of multiculturalism at her school. The teacher was sympathetic to the students' predicament, offering that it "takes a long time" to learn a new language and "is so difficult." However, she was also realistic about the fact that students did not do as well on standardized tests because they had not mastered English and did not have parents who could model English at home.

Likewise, a White teacher at a multiracial school acknowledged that the "community has made a difference" when asked how the neighborhood had affected her teaching. Yet, her language remained emotionally neutral when she described the ways she had to adjust her teaching because of her school's large immigrant population. She said:

> I find that there is a challenge with the language. I know very little Spanish but not to where it would be beneficial. Sometimes I need a translator to help out and if there is no one available sometimes I have to ask one of the students to help me out.

She adjusted to the language barrier by seeking students to translate for her in class. While this response may not be ideal pedagogically, at least she did not demonize the students for their barrier. She responded in a practical way to the parents' language barrier, too, by creating a standard form that parents could fill out when they had a question. Even this could be a challenge, however, because "parents are reluctant to write what they want because the language barrier is there. They may have the spoken language down but not know how to write it out." The teacher was familiar with the range of problems that the language barrier created and changed her practice in response to them.

Teachers treated the language barrier as a legitimate obstacle to student achievement and worked to overcome it. Racial match became important in this regard, because teachers who were former immigrants were sympathetic to students' struggles. A Middle Eastern teacher at a multiracial school commented that all but two students in his class were bilingual. When the interviewer asked if their English was "pretty good," the teacher responded:

> Yes, their English is pretty good. Sometimes they confuse their words because the two languages are different. Really small things. Like instead of saying "turn off" something they'll say "close." But I know what they're trying to say coming from a family that has experienced the same thing.

This teacher made a special effort to understand what his immigrant students were saying because he was familiar with translation problems. Similarly, a Latina teacher at a Latino school reported that she "broke out laughing" the first time she heard the expression "holy cow." As a result, she made it a priority to "connect the idioms with the stories" they read in class "because so much of their comprehension is based on understanding these little quirks of language."

Teachers viewed any progress students made in the face of the language barrier as a sign of their resilience. This was another benefit that immigrant minorities enjoyed because teachers believed their underachievement had a legitimate cause. An exchange with a Latina teacher at a Latino school illustrates this point. When the interviewer asked her, "Now what do you see as your students' strengths and weaknesses?" she replied:

> Well, because they're bilingual students I think because they're learning the English language and I think they're doing it very well, I think that just shows me that they're going to do okay. That they're going to be doing fine.

Rather than using the language barrier to lower her expectations, this teacher views her students' ability to learn English as a sign that they will succeed in school. A teacher who is Latina at the other Latino school saw resilience in her students' ability to overcome their parents' lack of involvement. She noted that English was not the first language of most parents. Because of this, she said, "I know that the work that the kids produce is totally from what they want to bring forth. I know that Mom and Dad are just going to say, 'Honey, please be good in school.'" She framed a deficit, lack of parental involvement, as causing a positive outcome, student self-sufficiency.

Implicitly, teachers constructed an economy of explanations for underachievement that delegitimized race and legitimatized ethnicity. This was evident when a Black teacher at a multiracial school said:

> I've seen a lot and you can mix cultures that are kind of on the same socioeconomic level and have at least some similar values but the problem with some of these really, really poor Black kids is that they don't even share my values. Plus they're not serviced at the rate they should be and okay, call me crazy, but when I can understand the Korean kid better than I can understand the Black kid don't you think you can give him some bilingual education maybe?

She constructed "Korean kids," who she "can understand" despite them being non-native English speakers, as being more deserving of aid than Black students. She insinuated that Black students, as native-born minorities, had no valid reason to have trouble speaking English, which ignores the structural barriers that these "really, really poor Black kids" faced. Moreover, she believed Black underachievement was caused by their values that were foreign to her. In this way, the teacher inverted the logic of the involuntary-immigrant minority split, constructing Blacks as the foreigners who "spoke funny" and Koreans as the familiar group. This is another example of teachers crediting students for ethnicized difference and penalizing them for racialized difference.

Unlike with Black students, teachers had a clear explanation for why immigrant students underachieved, which provided them with hope of improving their performance. They could afford to be optimistic because they thought they understood the problem. Teachers provided detailed diagnoses of their students' challenges and responded with concrete changes in their practice. Still, teachers may have over relied on the language barrier as an explanation for underachieving, with one teacher claiming that she "cannot differentiate" between the bilingual and non-bilingual students in her low-achieving class. Still, only a handful of teachers attributed immigrant underachievement to the disinterest or bad values of their parents, with most looking to the language barrier as the explanation.

Decent Immigrants. This narrative emphasized the positive values and morals that distinguished immigrant minorities from other racial/ethnic groups. Teachers ascribed pro-school values to Asians and Latinos and a mainstream morality evidenced by their two-parent family structure. Teachers also felt enriched by the students' ethnic difference. They cited community-mindedness, lack of materialism, and religiosity as virtues that made immigrant minorities unique. Moreover, many found the students' ethnic difference enriching. Still, teachers emphasized different parts of the decent immigrant narrative according to the race/ethnicity of the student. They were more likely to say Asians and White European immigrant students had an interesting culture, and more likely to construct Latinos as poor, but harmless and moral.

A common theme in interviews was that ethnicized minorities, particularly Asian students, had pro-school values. For example, a White parent-teacher association member at a multiracial school said that Korean parents "push[ed] their kids very hard to achieve in school." She believed that "all the immigrant groups here have a strong commitment to education because they see that as a ticket for their children into American society. It's the old story." Importantly, she credited Koreans as being part of the "old story," the one in which immigrants pull themselves up by their boot straps. The low achievement of native-born minorities such as Blacks undermined this American dream, but the success of immigrant minorities such as Koreans lent credence to it.

Moreover, teachers believed that immigrant parents valued education despite their own disadvantages. A Latina teacher, when asked about the parents at her Latino school, said, "There are some parents who value education and even if they're illiterate, their children do well. And the parent who doesn't value education, he could be middle class or poor, if he doesn't value education, the child does not do well at all." This teacher lauded poor Latino parents for not giving up on education as the path to mobility, even if they were uneducated themselves. In other words, she praised them for believing in the American Dream.

Teachers described the students as respectful, well-behaved, and able to get along with each other. When asked about the parents of her students, a Black teacher at a multiracial school said that "they're more respectful of teachers than the general population." Moreover, teachers thought immigrant minorities had traditional, well-functioning families. For instance, a Black teacher at a Latino school claimed "probably eighty-five percent of our kids do get supervision, positive supervision" at home. She went on to say:

> Our kids for the most part are very caring. They care about each other, they care about themselves, they care about their teachers. Just on any holiday, the gifts that we get are just unreal. And that shows us that our parents and students really do, not only do they like us, but they have more than an affection for us.

A White teacher at a multiracial school was also impressed with how caring her students were. She recalled how her class "clapped" when an Asian student, who came to the class not speaking any English, "started to raise (his) hand" and "did the math problem on the board . . . very easily." The students clapped spontaneously, "not because (the teacher) asked them. It was so sweet and cute." She concluded, "They really help each other very much."

In some cases, teachers thought the dominant culture could learn from the traditional values of immigrant minorities. When asked whether her leadership practices were affected by the community, this White assistant principal at a multiracial school replied:

> I would say yes, because with it being such a diverse community and with its traditional values that you would not find in another community it helps with discipline. . . . One of the complaints that I have to follow up on is that a few third-grade males said inappropriate things to another third-grade female student. They think nothing of saying that they liked the way she looked but culturally speaking it is improper for a male student to say that to a female student. I do not think that there was any profanity or any suggestive remark but the parent was unhappy about that.

Though the parents were stricter about behavior than the school, they helped the school maintain discipline. The assistant principal also noted the way immigrant parents deferred to teachers' authority, saying that "in this community the parents basically feel that the teachers are right and that their kids should listen (to) them."

Other teachers favorably compared immigrants to the normative middle-class student. A White teacher at a multiracial school did so when discussing how being "lower middle class" affected her students, saying:

> They have high family values, it's a trade with the lower income, they're raised differently than the rich kids where they get their own room when they are one, these kids are sharing a room until they leave the house, including

children who sleep in the living room with their grandma, their parents sleep in a room with the younger brother or sister. I think that gives them more of a bond with their family.

She seemed to question values that "the rich kids" were taught when they were allowed to "get their own room when they are one." In contrast, she believed immigrants increased family bonds by having to share rooms. While this might be a naive interpretation of the effects of being less well-off, the teacher nevertheless complimented immigrant students for making a virtue out of necessity.

Teachers praised Latinos in particular for being family- and community-oriented. A Black teacher at a Latino school said:

The Latino community really works together. They help each other, one person is not in need and another person doesn't know about it. They share, they really do a lot to help each other, help the children. There's organized babysitting and things like that. So I think, and there's an extended family, which in the United States, we don't see that anymore.

She approved of the way Latinos preserved the extended family that has been displaced in the United States. Similarly, a White teacher at the same school cited the fact that "the school gets flyers from different organizations within the community that are asking for families to come (on) field trips" as proof that Latinos are "community-oriented."

Teachers did not always directly connect their praise of immigrants to students' ethnicity. However, they did connect certain traits, like community-mindedness and lack of materialism, to students' ethnic heritage. These were all moral qualities. Thus, while teachers did not ethnicize all of the positive qualities of immigrants, they did ethnicize the factor that pushes them ahead of Blacks in their esteem, their decency.

Racial Narratives

Culture of Poverty. Teacher perceptions of Blacks illustrate racial narratives. The culture of poverty narrative combined themes of poverty and disadvantage, danger, morality, and community disorganization. The themes were similar to those for the ethnic culture of poverty, but were different in emphasis and tone. Teachers went into detail describing the social costs of poverty, befitting the greater emphasis on group fate in the Black narratives. More significantly, teachers treated poverty as a moral category, constructing students as having bad values because of it. This response was closer to the traditional definition of the culture of poverty.

Across schools, teachers described the dangerous and disorganized neighborhoods in which they perceived poor Black students to be raised. Many were sensitive toward students' social conditions, yet, their focus on social disadvantages sometimes displaced their educational mission. This Black principal at a Black school was keenly aware of all the social problems facing her students:

> You find that our kids are victims of racism, they're victims of poverty. They're just victims of so many illnesses. You see, we did some research on the crime rate. The crime rate is high. You can walk outside sometimes; you can see people out there selling drugs. You can see things that the kids are exposed to.

At times, her teachers "can't begin to deal with the literacy because something has happened in the community." She advised her faculty not to teach on those days, saying, "Sometimes teachers will come and say, 'Well should I go on and teach the lesson?' And I say, 'No you can't do that because you've got to deal with those issues with the kids.'" The principal's practice of treating students "holistically" meant that she focused on comforting students when violence erupted in the neighborhood. Still, schools had to take care to balance meeting their students' emotional needs with their academic mandate.

While correlates of poverty such as crime and violence inspired compassion, it also had the potential to drive teachers away. This almost happened to a Black teacher, whose first thought when she initially visited her future school was, "I'm looking at garbage and trash and crackheads at seven something in the morning. I said, no way am I going in this area to teach." In her eyes, the neighborhood was not just poor, its inhabitants lacked decency as evidenced by the "garbage and trash and crackheads" she saw. This version of poverty is in stark contrast to the way teachers constructed Latinos as weathering poverty with dignity. She was eventually won over by the excitement about learning she found at the school, but may not have made it that far if she had just gone by her initial impression.

Indeed, when teachers mentioned Black poverty, they often connected it with bad morals, especially as represented by dysfunctional families and non-normative family forms. This narrative differed from the ethnic culture of poverty, since teachers did not connect Latino poverty with the decline of the Latino family. For instance, when a Black teacher at a Black school was asked what percentage of her students came from two-parent families, she replied:

> Let's see, out of thirty kids, I'd say I have ten living with a grandparent or foster parent and twenty living with their mother. I think I only have one who lives with both parents. And those numbers are consistent with my class last year. Most of the boys, I only have nine boys in the class, have no male figure in their lives. It's really sad. Then there's the crack kids. Like Steve, for instance. His mother was doing crack when he was still inside her.

As this quote shows, many teachers believed that Black parents were uninvolved for illegitimate reasons such as drug addiction or non-traditional family structure. A White teacher at a Black school said:

> We are told to worry about test scores . . . you [the researcher] saw the problems I have in that special education class . . . you saw the fights . . . these are foster children where an outside agency is taking care of them.

This teacher believed that her students were too poorly behaved, due to their family backgrounds, for her to aim to raise their test scores. By lessening her responsibility for teaching these students, the teacher penalized Black students for violating mainstream family forms.

Teachers also faulted poor Blacks for violating gender norms, recounting tales of female-headed households, boys without male role models, and endangered Black men. There was no trace of this discourse in talk of Latino poverty. The belief that Black men and boys were in crisis was ubiquitous; it came up in several different schools. Teachers believed the crisis was important enough to dedicate resources to address the problems of Black boys. This was a clear example of the consequences of the culture of poverty narrative. Teachers reserved scarce resources for Black boys, which overlooked the fact that both Black boys and girls were underachieving.

Several of the Black schools instituted programs that were targeted to Black boys. The Black principal at one school started an after-school program where professional Black men mentored Black boys in reading. At another school, the Black principal explained how she convinced her skeptical faculty that they should initially restrict a new literacy program to boys. She recounted:

> They said, "Don't you think the girls are going to get upset?" They said, "We just don't like that." So I said, "You know what? In our area, where are our boys? The boys that leave here. What happens to them?" I said, "When we go to other places, where do we see them when we passed [the street the school is on]? What are they doing . . . standing beside the building, aren't they? So, don't you think we need to start now doing something for our boys?"

The principal repeated the key plot points of the "Black boys in crisis" narrative, which is that without proper guidance, Black boys will end up unemployed ("standing beside the building") or in jail. Teachers at her school came around to accepting this justification for limiting the program. When asked specifically about why the literacy program was limited to boys, a Black teacher said, "I think that the boys are really a group that does not read. When you get through motivated them, that girl is going to outread that boy every time."

Another teacher at the school picked up the crisis narrative, saying she, too, had wondered why the program was restricted to boys, but later decided:

> It's a little encouragement for them, "Do the right thing, stay on track." Because of course we lose so many men that are just out of the family, they're

just not around. And there's more women of course around here than men. So they just wanted to do something to pull the boys together, have them doing something that's positive. And saying if you're reading, if you're reading you're learning more and if you learn more, that will actually, hopefully give you incentive to go out and do something with your life. Because if you're not reading, a lot of our boys we lose them. Okay, if they're not reading they don't come to school, they don't perform. And then they're gone, and that's another one that's gone and that we've lost.

The teacher was concerned about the future of the Black community as a whole, not just the success of particular students at her school. Her fear of losing Black men to illiteracy fits with the crisis narrative that "we lose so many that are just out of the family." Like many Black teachers in the study, she slipped into using the possessive "we" when discussing Black students, indicating a belief that her fate was linked with that of her students.

Yet, the "Black boys in crisis" narrative is troubling for the way it envisions Black men as the salvation for the Black community. This type of thinking undervalues Black female achievement and overlooks their distress. Thus, the teacher remarked:

When you think about it the girls throughout the whole year they get little rewards and compliments and it's always the girls that are doing. And they're gonna do their work neat and they're gonna do, they're gonna overachieve. So if we pull the boys together and try to give them a little boost, that does something for their morale as well as them coming, making them want to come to school and do. And saying we believe in you, we want you to achieve, we're counting on you.

By saying that "we're counting on you," she hinted at the special role that Black men have in saving the Black community according to the culture of poverty narrative.

At-Risk Kids. Black underachievement, due to parents not valuing education and lack of parental involvement, drove the "at-risk kids" narrative. Teachers constructed Blacks as students who were far below average achievement, not just a little behind. Teachers using this narrative were vague about the causes of Black underachievement, except for lack of parental involvement, and did not talk about solutions much.

Teachers associated Black students with very low achievement. A Black teacher at a Black school complained that teachers were unfairly blamed for underachievement. She said, "The kids come in three years behind and other schools' kids come in where they should be. And so it's not bad teachers but it's, it's you have to deal with what you deal with." Moreover, Black underachievement seemed intractable to many teachers. A frustrated White teacher at a Black school said:

> We've got a binder about this thick with research that we've done trying to figure out, what is it with our kids? Why is it that we're putting forth all this effort and having so much of a problem with getting beyond, raising scores and making that just accelerating the learning for the kids?

While teachers of Latino students may have overemphasized the language barrier, teachers of Black students did not have recourse to that explanation for underachievement. In the absence of academic explanations, teachers who used the at-risk narrative often looked to social causes and solutions to Black underachievement.

A Black teacher at a Black school saw lack of parental involvement as the cause of Black underachievement. She said she needed parents to help their children with their homework, but:

> That's asking their parents to read that information that you've given them. And plenty of time their parents can't read and they can't comprehend what you're asking them. They can't. They just simply can't. And, in my opinion, I don't think the state of education in the inner city is going to get any better unless we get involved with what's going on at home because that's the only way; the only way I made it was with my parents.

The teacher was pessimistic about her students' achievement because they did not get the parenting she did. Her response was typical of Black teachers whose empathy for students due to racial match was tempered by the class difference they also felt. Both the class difference and the empathy borne from racial match were evident in a statement the teacher made in another interview. When the interviewer asked how she dealt with the lack of parental involvement, she responded that parents have to realize that her "goal is not necessarily to get [their child] to be a critical thinker."

> My goal is to get them to—they have so many social problems that lots of times I'm not going to teach them. Lots of times I'm not going to reach them. But if I teach them that here's a young, Black woman who's intelligent, she's serious, she treats me nice, she's always here for me when I need her— sometimes I think that's more important than making sure that they're scoring about grade level on the [(standardized tests)] because plenty of times, lots of these children are coming from homes with rats and roaches on the inside. So they don't care about the [standardized tests]. They care about, "At least I made it here today."

Her racial match, as a "young Black woman who's intelligent" fed into her desire to help her students. However, her students' class differences as individuals who came "from homes with rats and roaches on the inside" leveled her expectations of them. The phrase "rats and roaches" is important because it slips into labeling the students as unclean, which might be an indictment of their decency. Their race-class difference made teaching poor Black students futile. Ultimately, she sought to help students feel supported, not to help them to achieve.

Because parental involvement was so important to teachers, teachers' belief that Blacks have illegitimate reasons for being uninvolved affected their optimism about student success. The relatively new Black principal at a Black school advised her teachers to make the most of the time students spent in school, because they could not count on parental involvement at home. She said:

> And I explained to them that you have been here much longer than I have and you know the situation. You know that there are five or six children. You know there are only two or three bedrooms. There are plenty of people in and out of homes. You don't have that quiet time where you can sit at the kitchen table because there's no kitchen. There's a little cooking area, but no kitchen where maybe we sat at the table and did our homework while Momma cooked dinner. That's not happening. So you don't have a traditional family who is supporting education the way that most of our parents did.

Inadvertently, the principal revealed a double standard in how teachers treated racialized and ethnicized difference. If students needed private space such as a "kitchen table" to do their work, then teachers should have had low expectations of immigrant families who live in cramped quarters. Yet, it was not the fact of poverty, but racialized poverty that caused the principal to be pessimistic. She treated Black poverty as a moral category by implying that the lack of a "traditional family" interfered with their valuing of education.

Unlike with Latinos, these teachers blamed Black students for their underachievement by saying they did not value education. Racial match mattered in that teachers maintained responsibility for students despite their belief that they caused their own underachievement. Teachers expressed fatigue and incredulity at Black students' lack of educational achievement, but not the disgust they showed when talking about students' families and community.

Social Responsibility. This narrative emerged from teachers' sense of responsibility for students due to racial match. The narrative accords with research showing that Black teachers view teaching as a matter of social justice (Foster, 1998; Ladson-Billings, 1997). Teachers who used this narrative were not narrowly focused on student academic achievement, but on building a better future for Black students. Like the other two narratives about Black students, this narrative was mainly voiced by Black teachers. However, unlike in the other two narratives, teachers mentioned their similarity to as much as their difference from students. Black teachers' sympathy for their students was fueled by their shared experience with low teacher expectations and other disadvantages as children. These memories fostered a commitment to social justice.

Racial match was part of the reason that the Black assistant principal at a Black school maintained responsibility for her students. She was aware that Black students faced low expectations, even at her own school, because of their race and class. Because she faced similarly low expectations, she knew that her students were capable of more than what others expected. She said:

> I don't allow anyone to say to me "because he's this, because he's that, because he's the other he can't do it." The reason for that is you could have been talking about me, when I was that age. I know given time, resources, and proper teaching I can get it. I believe . . . we used to have it posted, if he didn't learn it, you have not found a way to teach it. I fondly believe that.

Racial match and a sense of injustice also fueled this Black teacher's commitment to Black students. She recalled that there was "no differentiation" based on race and class in the types of programs students received when she was a student in Laketown public schools. Yet, today things like "after-school programs" are restricted to:

> Only the faithful few. You know? Or only the chosen few are, not the faithful few, but the chosen few received the perks as they call it now. And I don't think it's fair. And I fight that whole mindset. I fight it in my classroom. I fight it with other teachers because I don't, I tell my children, I don't think there's anybody any better, any more intelligent, any smarter than you are. Especially when you come from a race of people that helped build the world. Give me a break.

She saw a clear line between the way schools hoarded "perks" for privileged students and the "mindset" that poor Black students are less intelligent than other groups. She racialized her high expectations when she asserted that her students "come from a race of people that helped build the world." She invoked the language of social struggle by saying she "fight(s)" against low expectations in her students and colleagues.

Nevertheless, a hidden penalty lurked within the social responsibility narrative. The penalty related to the way teachers cast Black families and communities as without strengths, which required the school to intervene. Often, teachers seemed to be trying to save Black students from their environment, including their families. Thus, the Black principal of a Black school said:

And what I found that—and getting back to my idea of being a role model, many of these children don't have role models, not to say *all* but they don't have the kind of positive role models that we know children need and should have that can help them to develop into the best that they can be. So the teacher may be the only role model. So we try to provide—we do provide many of the things that they do not get at home. Not everything, but I know we have to fill in the gap.

The notion that school has to "fill in the gap" is predicated on the belief that Black parents could not be proper "role models" for their children. Thus, the principal's abiding commitment to Black students came at the cost of viewing Black families as unable to support their children's education. In contrast, teachers of Latino students were able to see strengths within Latino families, even those who were not involved in school.

Black teachers evidenced the "lift as we climb" ethos characteristic of the Black middle class (Foster, 1998; Walters, 1999). Teachers at two of the seven Black schools explicitly linked their practice of taking students on college tours to their desire to uplift the race. One school made a point out of taking students on college visits to historically Black colleges. At another Black school, a Black teacher said, "I really feel like we have got to get our race of children, the bulk of them, attending college. . . . I don't see that these children are any dumber than anyone else. They lack opportunity." Later on, she linked her push for Black students to attend college with her own racial struggles. She said:

And I think that if we can get them, get more of them interested in education, that we would have more professional and successful people in the African American race. So I really do think that the purpose of the education is to continue the education until you become a professional. And then I think that would change our race altogether. . . . When I see as a poor girl what education did for my life I know that it could do it for some other child's life.

Her desire to increase the number of "professional and successful people in the Black race" exemplified Black teachers' wish to increase Black students' social mobility.

The fact that schools took Black students on college trips shows teachers' long-term investment in their students. Remember that these were elementary school students who had several years until college. Teachers wanted Black students to be successful in life, not just at school. When an interviewer asked the Black principal at a Black school, "What would you like to have [the students] to have . . . as they leave school?" The principal responded:

I want them to feel that if they apply themselves they can master the challenges that [are] present to them in society. When they're in high school as well as things that are just out there in the community. They can deal with the drug dealing and the gangs and that type of thing that goes on all around them. And survive not succumb to it.

Indeed, their commitment to redressing students' disadvantages sometimes overshadowed teachers' pedagogical responsibility. A White teacher at a Black school defended the amount of time her school spent improving her students' exposure to high-status knowledge and skills, or cultural capital (Bourdieu, 1984). She took her students to all of the "cultural events" she could "think of" to ensure "that they are exposed to some of the things that many of them" have not experienced. She knew that some people might say "they're spending too much time taking trips," but she saw the trips as "building background experience . . . that is so much more valuable when it comes to reading and writing." She believed this exposure would pay off academically, saying "if you read a story about a circus and you have never even been to a circus, you really have no connection. Or if you've never been to a forest preserve."

Likewise, a Black principal at another Black school knew that her students can "give you the rhythm," but wanted to expose them to "Bach or Mozart" and other music "they might not hear at home" to build their social "confidence."

Teachers who used the social responsibility narrative spoke concretely and in detail about Black kids' social disadvantages. It is likely that this interest in their students' future came from racial match. Teachers of Latino students did not dwell on their students' life after primary school because they did not link their fate to their students'. Teachers were knowledgeable about Black students' social problems, but they were knowledgeable about Latino students' academic problems.

WELL-MEANING CULTURAL TOURISTS AND FRUSTRATED NATIVES

Two ideal types, *Well-meaning Cultural Tourists* and *Frustrated Natives*, capture the differences in teacher response to ethnicized and racialized minorities. Well-meaning Cultural Tourists (WCTs) had benevolent, but shallow views of immigrant minorities. Teachers who were of a different race from their students and who taught at Latino or multiracial schools largely fell in this category. These teachers showed their benevolence by assuming the best about immigrant minority students. However, they were not interested in student outcomes beyond how they achieved and behaved at school. Instead, they were concerned about domains that directly affected them.

Moreover, Well-meaning Cultural Tourists only saw what they wanted about immigrant minority life, as tourists often do when visiting a foreign country. They did not show deep knowledge of immigrant minority students; instead they spoke in generalities that sometimes seemed derived from ethnic stereotypes. These teachers had a just-passing-through mindset in terms of how much they invested in students. They admired immigrant minority culture, but not enough to get involved in their lives outside of school or to help them with their future.

Black teachers responded to Black students from the perspective of being Frustrated Natives, that is, those who were native to Black culture but were frustrated by how their students manifested Blackness. Black teachers often expressed their views in stronger terms than the Well-meaning Cultural Tourists. Where the WCTs emanated general, distracted warmth toward immigrant minorities, Frustrated Natives raged at and rallied around the plight of Black students. They spoke more vehemently about both the good and bad of Black students. Their passion likely came from being insiders to Black culture, which was accompanied by a sense of possessiveness toward Black students.

Yet, Black teachers were not completely native to the Black student culture they encountered. They were distanced from their students by both class and generation. That distance was a source of frustration about where the students were compared to where they wanted them to be in terms of social mobility. Frustrated Natives were invested in their students' future, not just the present, because they felt that their fate was linked with their students'. Their interest was not only professional, but personal.

THE SOCIAL COST OF MINORITY STATUS

There was a decency gap in teacher perceptions of minorities. Teachers ascribed Latinos with decency, of not succumbing to the violence in their neighborhoods, being well-behaved, being community-minded, and family-oriented, that ennobled their difference. In contrast, they ascribed Blacks with moral deficits, particularly as related to non-normative family structure, that made their difference an obstacle at best or a permanent impediment at worst.

Teachers distributed symbolic resources to minorities unequally as a result of the distinctions they made. They rewarded immigrant minorities by maintaining expectations for achievement, giving them the benefit of the doubt about their lack of parental involvement, and being optimistic about their ability to overcome their language barrier. In contrast, teachers penalized Black students by lowering expectations, showing bad faith about their lack of parental involvement, and being pessimistic about their ability to achieve. In short, teachers created a symbolic economy where Latinos and Asians received ethnic credits and Blacks received racial penalties.

While there were disparities in the benefits minorities received for their difference, this disparity should be put in perspective. Credits and penalties are relative. In this study, ethnicized minorities had a relative advantage over racialized minorities in how teachers responded to them. Still, all things being equal, it would have been better for students to have been native-born, middle-class Whites.

Though some teachers were chastened by immigrant minority virtues, such as their family orientation, they were much more likely to reward them for having values that were similar to (not better than) the dominant culture. Teachers individualized immigrant minority struggles, making mobility a matter of individual virtues like maintaining dignity while poor, rather than something that required a structural response like implementing anti-poverty programs. Thus, the credits teachers awarded for ethnicized difference ultimately reinforced the status quo. Immigrant minorities' good values in the face of disadvantage meant that the dominant culture did not have to change.

If disparities in teacher perceptions of minorities ultimately served the status quo, how do we explain Black teachers' response to Black students? Recall that teachers responding to Latinos were likely White or otherwise racially mismatched with their students. This was not the case with perceptions of Black students, where teachers were more likely to be racially matched with their students. Black teachers' response shows how hegemonic negative perceptions of Blackness are. Even teachers who used the social responsibility narrative, and thus had more positive perceptions, constructed the Black poor as lacking and in need of rescue.

At one level, the negative perceptions seemed to be more about class than race. This is true, as far it goes, since the racial lens of social responsibility does not give Black teachers tools for thinking through Black poverty. Still, Black teachers' negative response to Black students was also about race, since Blackness is so fused with poverty in the American popular imagination (Pierre, 2004). Black teachers internalized the culture of poverty narrative, just as many other members of the middle class have, even though it results in problematic views of Blackness. Specifically, Black teachers internalized the idea that the Black poor had no strengths.

This may be the most far-reaching effect of the ethnic credit/racial penalty system, to render racialized groups valueless. After all, admiration implies perceiving something admirable, that is, something valuable within a culture. Black teachers felt many things toward Black students, empathy, alarm, indignation, but not admiration. Black teachers did not intend to do the bidding of White supremacy by buying into the culture of poverty narrative, but did so anyway. Thus, the symbolic economy seemed to create new winners and losers among minorities, but actually made it harder for any minority to combat White supremacy.

CHAPTER 3

Good and Bad Diversity

Judging Difference in
Multiracial Schools

I can't really pick it out for you anymore because it's even in my clothes. Now to school
I just wear a uniform but when I'm not wearing a uniform I noticed one day, I said,
"God, everything in my closet's from another country" 'cause I like Indian clothes and
I like Japanese clothes, and I've got stuff from Maui; it just happened. I became more,
not accepting, I was always accepting, it was okay then for me to wear it.

> —A Black teacher at Dodge (a multiracial school) talking about
> how she had been influenced by the diversity at her school

Teachers at multiracial schools expressed enthusiasm about their schools that was
unmatched by teachers at any other type of school in my study. They were particularly proud of the diversity of their student body and many said that they came to
their school *because* of its diversity. Yet, teachers at multiracial schools rarely talked
about native-born minorities when they described what they liked about their
school's diversity. In fact, teachers framed the benefits of diversity, such as exposure to foreign cultures, clothes, and foods, in a way that hinged on an encounter
with the "foreign." Thus, while teachers at multiracial schools consistently said
they were drawn to the diversity of their schools, they were selective about which
minority groups they praised.

This chapter explores what happens when teachers make distinctions between
good and bad diversity. Teachers judged the value of diversity on two levels: in
terms of how much they gained from interactions with minority students and in
terms of how much they had to accommodate diversity in their teaching. Diversity was valuable, not mainly because it was equitable, but because it benefited
the teachers. Their distinctions between minority groups reflected color blind
multiculturalism. Multiculturalism made teachers excited about the contact with
foreign cultures that was possible at multiracial schools, yet color blindness made
teachers overlook how Blacks contributed to diversity.

Teachers drew on productive diversity when making distinctions between minority groups. Productive diversity values diversity according to how it benefits the
dominant group rather than by how well it redresses minority disadvantage (The
New London Group, 1996). Teachers wanted to gain the benefits that came from

knowing about and interacting with foreign culture, that is, they wanted to earn multicultural capital (Reay et al., 2007). Specifically, teachers wanted the status that came from being seen as cosmopolitan and tolerant. Blacks, lacking an immigrant heritage and misconstrued as lacking ethnic difference, held little value in this definition of diversity. In short, teachers believed immigrant minorities constituted good diversity and native-born minorities constituted bad diversity.

The teacher whose quote begins this chapter illustrates these themes. She has internalized the value of multiculturalism so completely that it has affected how she dresses. However, she uses the ethnic discourse of cultural artifacts such as clothes when describing the positive aspects of diversity. Moreover, she says that all her clothes were "from another country," expressing an appreciation of foreignness that other teachers also report. Finally, she focuses on how diversity has benefitted her, saying that it has given her a chance to display tolerance.

The teacher shows the second aspect of assimilating diversity, focusing on how diversity benefits the dominant group. In this case, a Black teacher is an agent of dominant culture. She thinks in terms of what she gets from diversity, not in terms of what the dominant culture owes minority students. As we will see, this instrumental view of diversity creates blindness to the value of racialized minorities.

A MULTIRACIAL OASIS IN A SEGREGATED CITY: DODGE AND BOWEN ELEMENTARY SCHOOLS

Laketown is a very segregated city; so much so that residents use the side of town or the name of a neighborhood to signify the racial composition of an area. In fact, a resident could predict the demographics of the other nine schools that I studied just by hearing the name of the neighborhood where they were located. Dodge Elementary School and Bowen Elementary School were different. They were both located in one of the few integrated neighborhoods in the city. The schools were not just integrated, which conjures the image of two races living together; they were multiracial. The student bodies at Dodge and Bowen were comprised of significant percentages of three or more racial/ethnic groups (see Table 1.1). As compared to students of color (i.e. the total number of African-American, Asian-American, and Latino students), Whites were a numerical minority that comprised less than 45% of the student body at both schools. Teachers' response to the students at Dodge and Bowen was shaped by this contrast between the segregation of the city and the diversity of their schools.

The schools had a similar mix of racial and ethnic groups since they were located in the same neighborhood. Whites were the largest single racial/ethnic group at both schools followed by Latinos and Asians, then Blacks. However, as any teacher at these schools would tell you, the labels White, Latino, and Asian do not do justice to the diversity of the students. For instance, a significant number of the White students were not native-born, but recent immigrants from Eastern Europe. The Latino students were predominantly Mexican and Puerto Rican Americans, reflecting long-standing populations of those ethnic groups in the city. The Asian students were comprised of East Asians who had lived in the city for generations, such as Chinese and Korean Americans, and South Asians who had immigrated more recently, such as Indian and Pakistani Americans.

The diversity in heritage ended when it came to the Black students. Like most cities in the Midwest, the Blacks in Laketown were overwhelmingly native-born, not immigrant minorities. This lack of an immigrant heritage worked to the detriment of African Americans when teachers evaluated the diversity of their schools. As the quote that begins this chapter shows, teachers were drawn to the thrill of learning about foreign cultures. Teachers viewed Blacks as merely different, not foreign; learning about them was not akin to visiting a foreign country. Thus, a main theme of this chapter is the way teachers erased Blacks in their account of what made diversity at their schools good.

Moreover, Blacks were not the largest minority group at either schools; Latinos and Asians were. These demographics further distinguished the schools from the rest of Laketown, a city whose racial dynamics were still structured around the Black-White divide. For many teachers, these demographics, where the faces of minority students were Latino or Asian, not Black, and where diversity was the rule, not the exception, made Dodge and Bowen feel special. Teachers described the schools as utopian, almost places that were untouched by the racial tensions that haunted the city.

Both schools have gone through demographic transitions that changed the complexion of their diversity. The school's neighborhood had once been mostly Black and White; however, the schools had been predominantly White. The schools became more diverse in the 1980s, when South Asians and Latinos began to settle in the neighborhood. Interestingly, Bowen and Dodge never developed large populations of Black students from their neighborhood. Instead, many of the Blacks that attend the school today are bussed in from other areas. Eastern Europeans from the former Soviet Union are the newest immigrants to the neighborhood and have brought the newest wave of diversity to the schools. Finally, Whites and Asian-American students from other neighborhoods have been drawn to Bowen and Dodge because of their reputations as good public schools. Thus, the students are from both within and outside the neighborhood. Teachers who have been at the schools for a long time remember the different transitions and make distinctions between which waves constituted good diversity.

The teachers at Dodge and Bowen were much less diverse than their students (see Table 1.2). Whites were in the majority on the faculty at both schools, comprising 60% of the teachers at Bowen and 73% of the teachers at Dodge. A racial mismatch in which students are predominantly minorities and teachers are predominantly White is common in urban public schools (Frankenberg, 2006). Additionally, several of the White teachers in the study admitted to having little contact with people of color prior to coming to their schools, which is also typical of teachers in urban public schools (Frankenberg, 2006). Research has historically shown that White teachers have negative perceptions of schools when they are racially mismatched with their students (Alexander et al., 1987; Casteel, 1998). Surprisingly, the opposite was true at Dodge and Bowen, since many White teachers were attracted to their schools because of their diversity.

White teachers' perceptions were especially salient at the schools given their predominance; moreover, their enthusiasm about teaching students of color was unexpected given previous research. For these reasons, this chapter pays special attention to White teachers' beliefs about diversity. The response of teachers of color to multiracial schools, though also positive, was not as fervent as that of the White teachers. The White teachers seemed to be more affected by the symbolism of teaching at multiracial schools than teachers of color were. They also seemed more invested in the image of multiracial schools as oases of racial harmony in a segregated city. In short, White teachers' inexperience with students of color drew them to multiracial schools instead of driving them away.

"LOTS OF FLAVOR": THE ATTRACTIONS OF DIVERSITY FOR TEACHERS AT MULTIRACIAL SCHOOLS

"Interesting," "special," "new"—these were all words teachers at Bowen and Dodge used to describe why they chose to teach at a multiracial school. Teachers were attracted to the schools by the opportunity to interact with students who were different from themselves. The multicultural blend of their schools reminded them of the "United Nations," a fair-minded, cosmopolitan institution to which they felt privileged to belong. They were immersed in a noble project of bringing groups together and experiencing new culture.

But what kind of experiences did teachers seek to have? A White teacher at Dodge described being drawn to the school by a desire to be exposed to the unusual, the unfamiliar, in short, the foreign. When asked what she likes about Dodge, she said:

> Well I think that the best part and one of the other things besides the décor was that I liked the population. It would be something new to me. I just wanted to work with a diverse school that had lots of flavor and I've worked . . . in schools on the west side and . . . on the south side and this just seemed really appealing to me, so that's why I'm here.

This teacher's sentiment represented the view of the majority of teachers at multiracial schools. Teachers perceived multiracial schools as desirable places to teach *because* they were multiracial. This sentiment was especially evidenced by the fact that so many teachers cited the diverse student body as a main reason they decided to teach at multiracial schools. But the diversity they sought had to have "lots of flavor," a phrase that invokes the taste of foods that are unusual to Americans. Teachers wanted the diversity of cultural difference—of foreign clothes, values, and foods. Specifically, they wanted ethnic difference—that of White immigrants and immigrant minorities.

The teacher in the quote said as much though she used racial code words rather than racial and ethnic labels. She said she came to Dodge seeking students that were "new to" her, suggesting that she sought students of a different racial and ethnic background than herself. Yet, she narrowed the kinds of diversity that she sought, saying that she came to Dodge from schools on the west side and south side. In the racial geography of Laketown, "west side" and "south side" are code words for Black areas of the city. Reading between the lines, then, this White teacher sought a school with many different *foreign* races, not a predominantly native-born, minority school.

To illustrate these themes, I analyze many areas of teachers' discourse about their schools. First, I recount teachers' stories of how they came to teach at multiracial schools and discuss the role student composition played in their decision. Then, I describe the reasons why teachers had positive or negative perceptions of the schools and examine the distinctions they made between minority groups. Finally, I show that teachers' praise of multiracial schools is not solely altruistic, but motivated by productive diversity, that is, a concern with how diversity benefits them. This last point is amplified by a section on "diversity's discontents," in which I show that teachers supported diversity as long as it did not inconvenience them. Taken as a whole, I suggest that the "happy talk" of diversity discourse hides subtle distinctions that teachers make between minorities (Bell & Hartmann, 2007).

HOW TEACHERS CAME TO TEACH AT MULTIRACIAL SCHOOLS

Teachers at both multiracial schools told similar stories about how they came to teach at their schools. Even teachers who focused on the drawbacks of multiracial schools reported wanting to work there because of student composition. A comment by a White teacher at Dodge was typical. When asked how she would describe the students at the school, the teacher said: "Well I think they are very diverse. They come from all over the world which I think is really great. That was a selling point for me to come to this school."

Similarly, when asked what the students are generally like, a Black teacher at Dodge said, "There's no 'in general' and it's actually in a way the school I always dreamed of and I guess it's why a temporary position turned into a permanent one." She went on to say, "I didn't know that a place like this in [Laketown] existed because I was just used to places where I grew up where it was all one race and changing. . . . And when I came here I thought, 'This isn't gonna last' but it's really wonderful what's going on here right now."

This last comment by the Black teacher at Dodge suggests that teachers choose to come to multiracial schools due to their personal experiences with race. Other teachers' stories about how they came to teach at a multiracial school reflect this theme. For instance, a White teacher at Dodge told the interviewer that:

> I really didn't switch schools because I was so dissatisfied with the other two schools I was at. But the other two schools were composed of one type of student, one race. My first ten years I never saw anything but a Black kid in ten years, my second ten years I never saw anything but a Puerto Rican kid for ten years, and this school I think I have eleven different languages in my class so you're teaching all different kinds of kids and you're learning as you're teaching. You're learning about their ways.

He went on to tie his appreciation of this multiracial school to his own schooling experience: "I went all the way through private education so I only know a White-type of kid. I never had any friends who were Black or Puerto Rican or anything other than what I am so I am learning as we go at the same time with these kids." This teacher values the students that he teaches because they are different from him, reflecting multiculturalism's call to learn about other racial and ethnic groups. However, his comments also reveal his ultimate dissatisfaction with the segregation that he encountered at his two previous schools: He was ready to move on to a multiracial school, not just a minority one.

GIVING DIVERSITY ITS DUE:
PERFORMING COSMOPOLITANISM AND TOLERANCE

Teachers' praise for the school composition at multiracial schools often seemed ritualistic, since teachers at both Bowen and Dodge talked about the diversity in such similar manners. Specifically, many teachers mentioned the diversity of their student body at similar points during their interviews, highlighted similar characteristics and used the racial code word "diverse" when talking about their schools. The support for this last point is overwhelming; teachers used the word "diverse" in 49% of the interviews (20 of the 41 interviews).

By calling teachers' praise of diversity ritualistic, I do not mean to imply that it was insincere. Rather, I intend to point out that the phrasing and timing of their praise so closely matched each other as to seem impelled by a force greater than the individual teacher. The social norm of multiculturalism was likely the force that made teachers' praise so similar. Teachers' comments consistently showed respect for the same aspects of diversity, those that conformed to America's ideal of racial and ethnic harmony. Other scholars have found that teachers conventionally praise those aspects of diversity that prove that America can achieve unity within its multiculturalism (Olneck, 1990).

Teachers showed their concern with social norms when they reported on how other people reacted to the diversity of their schools. For instance, they talked about how a friend or a spouse also responded positively to the diversity of their schools. These absent witnesses to diversity were like the chorus in plays who represent what the common person is thinking. The approving voice of this chorus was a rhetorical device teachers used to show that their views were in the mainstream. Teachers' use of the chorus also reflected their concern with conveying a persona of being tolerant and cosmopolitan to an audience. Their response to the interviewers' questions was another chance for them to display this persona. Teachers did not just want to be tolerant and multicultural; they wanted to be *witnessed* being tolerant and multicultural.

Ritually Praising Diversity: Conventions of Diversity Discourse

Most teachers mentioned the demographic composition of their students at similar points in their interviews. Typically, teachers brought up the diversity of their schools when they were asked about the strengths of their school or of the school's neighborhood. Indeed, often one of the first things teachers praised about the school or community was its demographic composition. The exchange in the following interview was typical. The interviewer asked a White teacher at Bowen, "What's it like to work here?" Immediately after citing her colleagues as one of the things she enjoyed about her school, she said "And I also love the kids. They're so diverse and some of them are so innocent because, they've been in this little cultural bubble and they haven't seen the evils of the world too much and I love that."

Teachers also ritually praised the same characteristics of students. Once the topic of the diversity was introduced, most teachers went on to list the number of ethnicities present or languages spoken at their schools. If the teacher did not offer this information on her or his own, the interviewer would often elicit it by seeming impressed by their school's diversity. At Bowen, an interviewer mentioned having recently observed a Russian bilingual class at the school, saying "Yeah, I was in one the other day, it was just so interesting—I had never thought . . ." To which the White teacher responded,

And of course along Shepherd Lane you have a lot of the Pakistani Indian businesses, so naturally many of those children come here, and there's a lot of Assyrian population, the four major languages in the neighborhood are Russian, Assyrian, Burdo, and Spanish, and then there's a multitude of other East European languages, other Asian languages. So we used to have a much larger Korean population than we have now.

Here, the interviewer's interest in the diversity of the school prompts the teacher to go into greater detail about the languages spoken in the neighborhood.

Teachers also detailed their students' ethnicities and nationalities. In another interview at Bowen, the interviewer asked a White teacher, "So what nationalities are represented in your class?" To which the teacher replied, "I have Indian, Korean, Japanese, Spanish in terms of Mexican, Puerto Rican, some from El Salvador, African American, White." Similarly, a Black teacher at Dodge told her interviewer when asked what the "typical" child at the school was like, "I was taking a course and I had collected attendance books from about eight teachers and I ended up listing about fifty countries as places of birth. It's incredibly diverse so there's no typical . . . child." Again, this teacher's ritualistic enumeration of difference was said in the context of her praising the school because of its diversity. However, her focus on country of origin disadvantages—Blacks because their nationalities as Africans were deliberately erased during slavery.

This last finding, that teachers list the ethnicities and languages spoken by their students, yielded another important observation—most teachers used an ethnic discourse to describe the composition of their schools. While both multiracial schools contained involuntary minorities such as Blacks and Mexican Americans as well as immigrant minorities such as Asian Americans, teachers tended to reference only immigrant minority groups when discussing their schools' diversity. Although teachers could potentially laud all non-Whites as signs of diversity, in practice they tended to cite the presence of White European immigrants such as Russian immigrants, and immigrant minorities, particularly Asian groups, as the source of diversity in their schools.

For example, when an interviewer at Dodge commented to an Asian teacher that the school was "so diverse" the teacher replied:

Teacher: I think I have three kids that are American, maybe even two, no I have three.
Interviewer: Is there also a Hispanic population here?
[. . .]
Teacher: Yeah there are Hispanics, but most are Indian, Pakistani, Syrians, Yugoslavians, and lot of Russian and Mexicans. There are Asians but they are mostly Vietnamese or Philippine, rather than Chinese and Japanese.

For this teacher, diversity called to mind the school's various Asian and European ethnic groups, not Latinos.

Teachers often noted how the outside world responded to the diversity of their student body during their interviews. This suggested that they were somewhat aware that they were adhering to a social norm when they valued the diversity of their students. Teachers invoked the approving voice of this chorus to show that their views about diversity were widely shared. A White teacher at Dodge illustrates this point. He said of the diversity in his school:

> And it's a terrific thing. It's what the school is all about. People come here and they see our school, and that's the first thing Suzanne [his wife] noticed when she showed up here. "Oh, my gosh look at all these faces."

Similarly, an Asian teacher at Dodge observed, "With this city school we have [a] multicultural [population]. My friends are amazed when I tell them how many ethnic groups I have [in my class]." The positive reactions of the absent "wife" and "friends" invoked by these teachers stand in for the positive perception of diversity that they expect from the rest of society. However, the fact that teachers needed to invoke this imaginary chorus to buttress their own views suggests that multiculturalism is still not a settled social norm.

Good and Bad Diversity: Distinguishing Between Minority Groups

Teachers had definite views on which minorities groups constituted good and bad diversity at their schools. Sometimes this hierarchy of minorities came out when they directly compared groups of students. Recall the White teacher at Bowen who gushed about the diversity at her school, saying:

> And I also love the kids. They're so diverse and some of them are so innocent because they've been in this little cultural bubble and they haven't seen the evils of the world too much and I love that. And even some of the 8th-graders are still pretty innocent.

However, she was not as inspired by Black kids, saying, "Some of the kids have, unfortunately, seen too much but it's so different from my work as Grant Elementary . . . working with inner-city kids who've unfortunately seen too much." "Inner-city" is a racial code word for Black, so the teacher was essentially comparing immigrant minorities to native-born minorities. She found the innocence of immigrant minorities refreshing exactly because she was disheartened by the hardness of Black students she taught at Bowen and at her previous school. In short, she saw her school in terms of good and bad diversity, where some minorities are inspiring while others are dispiriting.

Teachers were most likely to reveal the hierarchy by which they ranked minorities when discussing changes in the student demographics over the years. Two stories about reactions to the demographic transition changes at Bowen illustrate the gap between how teachers viewed immigrant and native-born minorities at multiracial schools. The stories show that when teachers did mention involuntary minorities, they typically did so in the context of describing how the student body has changed for the worse. The White principal at Bowen revealed that his school violated efforts at integration prior to his arrival by trying "to actively recruit Korean-American (and) Chinese-American kids," but no other minority students. He tried to reverse this violation when he came to the school by recruiting minorities from a range of racial and ethnic backgrounds.

However, a Black instructional leader reported that parents saw the move to include non-immigrant minorities as a descent into bad diversity. She noted:

> There was a big change in the demographics in this school. The student population was soaring. The economic status of the school community was changing. It was declining. Every year we had more and more students who were qualifying for free and reduced lunches. That is the standard by which they judge the school's economic status. The ethnicity was changing. There were all these things that were changing and [the principal] was getting a lot of the blame for things that were not going right.

These new students were poorer and of a different ethnicity than previous waves of students. Both parents and teachers associated this demographic shift with lower achievement. The instructional leader went on to say:

> People that were teachers here long before I came but who were still here when [the principal] came were used to the upper-middle-class community with high-achieving students. When things started changing I think that rather than acknowledging the change in the students they were looking at [the principal] as being the problem. It just coincided.

Here the instructional leader defends the principal by blaming the influx of new students as the cause of the decline. However, we know from the principal's comments that the school was not opposed to all attempts to diversify the student body, since they were eager to recruit Asian-American students. Thus, the parents and teachers were against the diversity brought by the latest wave of minorities.

A pattern emerges if we put together the stories told by the principal and the instructional leader. We see that Bowen has a strong preference for immigrant minority students, whom they associate with high achievement, and a resistance to native-born minorities, whom they associate with poverty and low achievement. These stories show that teachers do think in terms of good and bad diversity and distinguish between minority groups on that basis. Further, teachers were willing to act on these distinctions and violate the rules of the school district to achieve what they perceived as good diversity. While teachers at Dodge had similar misgivings about the demographic transition at their school, they did not go to similar lengths to recruit the "right" kind of minorities. However, these two stories from

Bowen show that teachers' disparate perceptions of minorities can go from being private biases to being the basis of school policy if they are left unchecked.

BENEFITING FROM DIVERSITY:
PRODUCTIVE DIVERSITY AND MULTICULTURAL CAPITAL

Teachers at Dodge and Bowen were united in their praise of the diversity at their schools, yet their praise did not extend to all minority groups. Specifically, they overlooked or devalued the way Blacks contributed to diversity. I suggest this oversight was guided by color blind multiculturalism, which devalues minorities identified with racial difference. Teachers simply did not see how Black students, as native-born minorities, benefitted them in a symbolic economy that was preoccupied with "foreignness." In the next section, I home in on this notion of productive diversity by describing what teachers gained from teaching at multiracial schools. Specifically, teachers liked multiracial schools because they gave them the chance to teach about tolerance and difference, learn about the other, and prove that pluralism works. However, teachers' emphasis on what they gained from diversity made them undependable allies, who were less enthusiastic about immigrant minority students when they had to adjust their teaching to accommodate them.

Teaching About Tolerance and Difference

One reason teachers perceived multiracial schools as desirable was because its diversity gave them a chance to teach tolerance. Teachers viewed the diversity of their students as a resource because it made their lessons on tolerating difference more relevant. They often incorporated information about minorities into their curriculum as a part of these lessons on difference. Teachers seemed equally as motivated by the chance to expand their teaching repertoire as by the obligation to meet the needs of a diverse population.

Often teachers expressed their desire to teach about tolerance and diversity when interviewers asked them about their general teaching practice. An interview with a White teacher at Dodge offers one example. When asked if there was anything she was changing about her art teaching this year, the teacher replied that she was planning to do "more multicultural projects." She went on to explain,

> I think it's something very important and I think that it's one of the focuses in our school just because we are so diverse, we're lucky to have 1st-generation, 2nd-generation kids which demanding perspectives that I think that they deserve to . . . be part of this global understanding and I think art is really conducive to that.

This teacher's comments show that she thought the diversity of her students was an asset to her school and felt compelled to honor that asset by having a curriculum that represented the diversity of her students.

Similarly, a White teacher at Dodge spoke of how her students' diversity made her social studies curriculum especially relevant to them. When asked to describe her students, she called them "wonderful," saying:

> I love teaching this student body. They're so diverse. And from the perspective of a social studies teacher you couldn't ask for a better mix. I've got every country in the world here. And the issues of tolerance and understanding, we were talking today about xenophobia, fear of foreign people and objects. How we've had those periods where we've closed our doors to people coming in because we feared the unknown. And it's really wonderful to be able to work with a group like this because they're very understanding and I think very accepting of one another.

For some teachers, an added benefit of teaching at a multiracial school was that it gave them a chance to teach about their own ethnic background. When asked about her students' strengths, a White teacher at Bowen of Italian heritage remarked, "We're very diverse culturally. There's so much that we can do in terms of all the different languages. Sometimes I even start just to get their attention, just start speaking Italian." Meanwhile, at Dodge a native-born White teacher told the interviewer, "Our Russian Jewish teachers here have been very strong in teaching the Holocaust, it's very much a part of their culture and their religion and it's not something I have a vast knowledge of. So it's nice to take advantage of it." In both of these instances, the multiracial student body gave teachers a chance to teach about and display their ethnic difference from the White, Anglo-Saxon, Protestant norm.

Learning About the Other

A few examples from Dodge illustrate that teachers valued their student body because they provided them with a chance to learn about the other and thus gain multicultural capital. An Asian teacher explained that, "I even learn from them. I have learned more since I have been teaching. Learned how to teach and my methods have changed and some of my beliefs. I know how to work with them better." Her statement that she "even" learns from her students indicates that she had not expected to learn from them.

In a similar vein, a White male teacher at Dodge said, "The kids give it a definite plus of the school, the type of kids you teach, and each nationality is actually different, and it erased a couple of generalizations that I had about certain nationalities since dealing with the kids here." Finally, a Black teacher at Dodge showed her knowledge of differences among Asian ethnicities, saying "Vietnamese, you never pat them on the head because it's like a religious thing, nothing's supposed to touch their head but god," and, "It's quirky what not to do to the Japanese, what not to say to the Japanese. These people might seem like they're being really standoffish and snotty but you just seem like a freak 'cause you're telling all your business to somebody you hardly know 'cause you're an American." In all these examples, teachers positively perceived the ethnic composition of their school because of what they could learn from their students.

Proving that Pluralism Works

A final reason teachers gave for finding multiracial schools desirable is that the schools showed that pluralism works. As Tyack (2003) points out, America is constantly trying to convert the social reality of being a pluralistic society into a political reality of there being cooperation among groups. Thus, America is concerned with having the pluralism on the ground reflect the pluralism of its ideals. Often teachers lauded multiracial schools specifically for their racial harmony between students. In doing so, teachers were valuing the schools not only for embodying the ideal of pluralism, but for manifesting color blindness. This focus on racial harmony stood out since it was one of the few times when they switched to a racial discourse. As we see in the following section, teachers' celebration of the racial harmony between students provided the strongest evidence that they attributed to multiracial schools social value because of the symbolism of their school composition.

At both schools, many teachers mentioned the harmony between students as something that made their schools desirable. For instance, when asked to describe the school's neighborhood, a White teacher at Bowen said, "It's a diverse neighborhood that I really appreciate I really value the fact that so many of the kids come from different backgrounds and not second-generation, a lot of these kids just got to America and they form friendships across ethnic lines, religious lines." This teacher explicitly used the word "value" to describe how she felt about the intercultural friendships her students developed.

As I discuss below, teachers seem especially worried that their schools not be perceived as having racial conflict. However, they also wanted their schools to seem tolerant of ethnic differences, such as language and religion. They cast student conflicts as being grounded in individual characteristics, not group status.

A White teacher at Dodge does this when describing the case of an Asian-American student who had been having trouble fitting in with her fellow students. He raises then abandons group status as the cause of meanness toward immigrant minority students:

> There's a couple of kids that, it could be cultural, it could be, I mean kids are mean, kids are mean. They'll pick any, it could be the language, it could be the

way they dress, it could be because of glasses, it could be they're pudgy. Kids are mean to other kids, so sometimes kids become introverted because they don't want to be laughed at or made fun of.

This teacher starts to say kids are teased because of being immigrants, but that goes against the image ethnic tolerance that he wants to paint. Instead, he de-ethnicizes the issue and treats teasing for pudginess as equivalent as teasing for speaking with a foreign accent.

Often teachers spoke of the harmony between different social groups as un-expected, but welcome. A White teacher at Dodge illustrated the unexpectedness of harmony between students when she said:

> I think it's extremely unique to the city and it amazes me how well people tend to get along with each other. And I think these children—and I keep trying to tell them, don't realize how fortunate that they are that they're experiencing this now while they're growing up because I think it's going to help them become more tolerant and understanding and more educated because we learn about everybody's culture, whereas if we didn't have the different ethnic groups we wouldn't.

This teacher offers her school as embodying America's ideal of being a land where groups are able to learn about other cultures and become more tolerant. She de-scribes her students as being "fortunate" to learn in such a place, lending all the more value to multiracial schools for being some of the rare places where this ideal can be achieved.

While the previous teachers used the language of ethnic difference, citing cooperation among religious and ethnic groups to describe the harmony they perceived, other teachers' language drew on racial discourse. These teachers' com-ments showed their concern with the possibility of having racial, not just ethnic, harmony. The fact that teachers mainly did not use racial discourse until now is significant. It suggests that teachers associate race with conflict and other poten-tial drawbacks of diversity. Note that we have seen teachers mention Blacks, the most racially marked minority, only when talking about bad diversity or to over-look their contributions to good diversity. Thus, it is consistent with that pattern of associating race with bad diversity that teachers would only turn to racial discourse when talking about their concerns about diversity.

I quote the next few examples extensively to give the flavor of their attention to racial conflicts borne from diversity. A White teacher at Bowen discussed race relations when asked to describe her school's neighborhood. She said:

> I think for the most part it works well together and for the most part you don't hear of any racial conflicts with the kids or in the community, I mean different things happen but very seldom is it viewed as racially motivated

and I think that is really . . . valuable to have the kids growing up in an environment like this.

While this teacher admits to there being conflicts in the community, she is quick to note that the conflicts are "very seldom" viewed as being racially motivated. Her comments reflect color blind ideology in that she dismisses or finds illegitimate claims that racism could be fueling the conflict between groups. Observe, too, that she believes it is desirable for minority students to grow up in such an environment, suggesting that this teacher views the harmony as valuable because it confirms her color blind ideology.

Later in the interview she considers the racial harmony in the school itself, saying:

> You know I don't even think that the kids even think about it. They don't because when I see groups of kids in my class there are four kids who are really close, they are tight. One is a Syrian, one is Philippine, one is African American, and the other one is Jewish and they are the Four Musketeers, they are always together, everything they have to do together and all of the kids intermingle, and I don't think they even think about it. It's almost as if no one ever told them that there was something wrong with that.

Here, her statement that "no one ever told them that there was something wrong with that" is telling because it shows skepticism about multiculturalism and color blindness. This teacher knows that race still matters, which is why she is surprised that the interracial group of friends that she described exists. Her belief that groups intermingled across races was undermined by her need to tell the story of the Four Musketeers in the first place. What the teacher meant to be taken as the rule comes across sounding like the exception, or at least an exaggeration.

A White teacher at Dodge reflects the same concern with racial conflict between students and makes a similar assertion of racial harmony. When asked to describe the students at his school, the teacher replied:

> The surprising thing I found out, which I didn't think would happen, dealing with this many different races, there are not a lot of problems at this school. Hardly any, I find that each one of the races find that there are so many out here. If another student doesn't like another student, it's usually because they don't like the other student. It's not because of their race, and that is a surprising thing that I found out that I really like. Everyone pretty much gets along, although there are different races.

As in the previous example, this teacher's surprise at the racial harmony that he observed undermines his expressed confidence in that racial harmony. Here again is the unwillingness to believe that race could be a cause of conflict between students, a color blind belief. He draws on color blind discourse by asserting that conflict between students is based on individual not racial animosity. Here, too, we find that this teacher values a diverse student body for making America appear to live up to the pluralistic ideal of cooperation between races.

These examples show that teachers are aware that racial conflict can be a potential by-product of diversity. However, they believe diversity can transcend racial conflict. Teachers use rhetorical devices in their comments to bolster their claim that racial harmony is possible. A main strategy is to qualify their claims to make them sound reasonable given the history of racial conflict in Laketown and in society. For instance, the teacher at Dodge acknowledges the reality of racial conflict by saying he was "surprised" that more of it did not happen at his multi-racial school. This makes him seem more trustworthy when he claims that "hardly any" racial conflict occurs at his school. His comments convey that he knows that racial strife exists, but it was rare at his school.

DIVERSITY'S DISCONTENTS

For many of the teachers at Dodge and Bowen, there was no downside to diversity, only upsides. They were drawn to multiracial schools by what they could gain from them: practice at teaching with a multicultural curriculum, a chance to learn about foreign cultures and earn multicultural capital, and proof that our diverse society can achieve racial and ethnic harmony. Teachers had an instrumental approach to diversity that emphasized how multiracial schools served their needs. Indeed, this chapter is testament to the success of color blind multiculturalism in imbuing interactions with and knowledge of immigrant minorities with value.

Yet, teachers' response to immigrant minorities was not all positive. For one thing, some Black teachers were unaffected by the pull of diversity discourse. These teachers did not view immigrant minorities as bad diversity; rather, they were indifferent to the diversity at their schools.

Additionally, a number of teachers valued what they gained from immigrant minority students, but seemed somewhat burdened by the demands of teaching them. Teachers at both Bowen and Dodge expressed reservations about the cost of teaching such a diverse population. They often prefaced their complaints with praise of diversity, showing how dominant a norm that multiculturalism was at the schools. The teachers nevertheless expressed concerns about bilingual education for being time-consuming and confusing to administer, unnecessary or overused, and inconvenient for non-bilingual education teachers.

Dissenting Voices from Black Teachers

While teachers across races said that they were attracted to their schools be-cause of their diverse student bodies, a handful of Black teachers did not express this view. These Black teachers expressed reactions to the diversity of multiracial schools that ranged from indifference to disappointment. For instance, the Black assistant principal at Bowen, who is from Laketown, said that earlier in her career the school district forced her to stop teaching at her all-Black alma mater so that she could teach at a multiracial school. She explains that though she "really wanted to stay" at her old school, she had to transfer to a school "further northwest" because the school board wanted to "enhance integration" at Laketown schools. This teacher was not drawn to a multiracial school because of its diversity; in fact, she would have preferred to stay at an all-Black school.

Similarly, an interviewer asked a Black teacher at Bowen if she chose the school "Because you heard good things about it?" She responded, "No, because it was out of the area where I was working. Because I worked mostly in Black neighborhoods because I live far south and I wanted to change." This teacher's response indicates that she was not drawn to Bowen because of its diversity or anything else, but instead she sought to leave the orbit of Black schools where she had taught. While she did not feel a pull toward Black schools, as the assistant principal did, she certainly did not feel drawn toward multiracial schools, as the White teachers in the earlier examples did.

I recount the dissenting narratives of these Black teachers to suggest some limits to the appeal of multicultural ideology. While these two teachers' indifference to the appeal of multiracial schools was a minority sentiment, their response suggests that racial identity might play a yet unexamined role in teacher perceptions. While all teachers are subject to the social norm of multiculturalism, White teachers might be the most likely to express their appreciation of ethnic difference. Whites are more likely than people of color to have grown up racially isolated due to de facto segregation.

As the story of the teacher who went to an all-White private school suggests, this racial isolation might increase the appeal of multiracial schools for White teachers even beyond the usual value afforded to ethnic difference under multiculturalism. Indeed, recent research shows that Whites in particular choose to talk about celebrating diversity to signal their tolerance of difference, yet avoid talking about racial inequality (Pollock, 2004). A corollary to this finding is that teachers of color might be less influenced by the appeal of ethnic difference, all things being equal, because they do not have to prove their racial tolerance.

Burdened by Bilingual Education

A few examples illustrate these concerns about diversity. A White teacher from Dodge expressed reservations about the increasing immigrant population. She listed the rate of change at Dodge as a "challenge," saying:

I think we will always face the issue of the revolving door of students. Of changing student demographics. And I think that's a lot of what teachers react to. . . . Even though this is a fairly diverse school, but the characteristic of the diversity is changing over the past five years. So teachers are continually having to learn new cultures and deal with different cultural differences.

This teacher suggests that teachers cannot keep up with the rate of new groups of immigrants that come to the school. In other parts of the article, teachers talked about the pleasure they took in learning about new cultures. However, the process of gaining multicultural capital could become a burden if teachers did not have enough time to familiarize themselves with new groups.

Other teachers raised concerns about bilingual education. The next comment, which comes from the White teacher who told the story of the Four Musketeers at Bowen, shows the complex impact that diversity had on teachers. She valued her diverse school for fulfilling the ideal of racial harmony, but found that the diversity sometimes made it harder for her to teach. For instance, she always had to ask about how to adapt new curriculum so that it could be used with non-native English speakers:

> There is really no solution really given and when we go to faculty development workshops at [a college in Laketown] about the connected math we always bring it up, "What about the kids who don't naturally speak English, who are just learning how to speak English?" It [is] difficult and with such a diverse population and community of immigrant families it is difficult.

By her earlier remarks, we know this teacher enjoyed the diversity of her school. Yet, these later comments show her diverse student population made it harder for her to find materials to use with her students.

Similarly, a White teacher at Dodge was exasperated by the process of administering standardized tests to bilingual students. The presence of immigrant students meant that she had to keep track of different categories of children, because they were exempt from some tests but not others. Like the teacher at Bowen, we see this teacher weighing the benefits of teaching at a diverse school against the reality of changing her practices to fit them. She had taught previously at another multiracial school, ". . . but this one is very heavily diverse, multi-ethnic and the bilingual aspects and who tests, who doesn't test, who's involved in which program. I mean it's . . . very complex." The process of figuring out which students take the test was time-consuming, requiring "almost a full week solid just preparing for the tests in terms of going through class lists, eliminating kids." The teacher liked teaching at multiracial schools, having taught at one before, but found the process of testing bilingual children burdensome.

ADDING IT UP: BALANCING THE COSTS AND BENEFITS OF DIVERSITY

Teachers saw multiracial schools as desirable for three main reasons: because they gave them the chance to teach about tolerance, to learn about difference, and because they provided proof that pluralism works. These first two reasons reinforce the general finding of this chapter, which is that multiculturalism gives difference a positive charge that it did not have under assimilationist thought. This was especially evident from the fact that some teachers were able to perceive ethnic difference as improving rather than hindering their ability to teach.

The third reason teachers gave for finding multiracial schools desirable, because multiracial schools prove that pluralism works, speaks directly to the way teachers constructed multiracial schools as socially valuable. Teachers lauded schools in which they perceived students of different races and ethnicities as getting along. In this way, teachers attributed to multiracial schools embodiment of the pluralistic ideal that all groups would be able to cooperate without conflict. Hence, teachers mentioned the racial harmony they saw at their schools as one of their assets.

While teachers' talk about multiracial schools typically reflected an ethnic discourse, their discussion of the harmony between groups was one of the few places where they employed a racial discourse. For instance, many teachers specifically used racial categories instead of ethnic ones when they described the groups that got along at their schools or when they mentioned that racism was not occurring at their schools despite their multiracial student body. This theme suggests that color blind ideology was also at work in their evaluation of what made multiracial schools desirable, since the racial harmony they celebrated proved that racism that was no longer a force in society.

This chapter shows that productive diversity motivates teachers to value some minority students, but not others. White teachers' appreciation of multiracial schools was particularly surprising, given their historical negativity toward schools with large numbers of students of color. This positive view of diversity is a welcome change from the past, especially as minorities continue to grow as a segment of the public school population. However, teachers separated minorities into good and bad diversity, according to which minorities benefitted them the most. Teachers also expressed concerns about the changes they had to make to accommodate their bilingual student body. These concerns suggest that teachers had a more nuanced view of immigrant minorities than their praise of diversity suggested.

CHAPTER 4

"Kids Are Just Kids"
Managing the Stigma
Against Black Schools

"How does it feel to be a problem?" DuBois asked in his seminal work, *The Souls of Black Folk* (DuBois, 2007). Teachers at Black schools knew the feeling of being seen as problems better than most. They taught at schools that were constantly attacked for failing and thus making America less globally competitive. Compounding the stigma of failure was the stigma of teaching Blacks, a demonized minority group. When teachers entered a Black school, they entered a mythical place, one fixed in the American imagination as a space of lack, disadvantage, and even inferiority. Black schools existed under a cloud of negative perceptions that unavoidably affected the way teachers viewed them.

It is no wonder, then, that teachers had very different perceptions of Black schools than of multiracial schools. In the minds of many teachers, multiracial schools represented America's future. Teachers at multiracial schools were excited to talk about what they had learned from their students and were proud to be associated with the project of multiculturalism. They believed that multiracial schools embodied some of America's greatest ideals: progress, harmony, and tolerance.

If multiracial schools were America's future, then Black schools were ugly reminders of America's past. They represented all that America had failed to overcome: segregation, disadvantage, and underachievement. Teachers were wary of Black schools; instead of being excited, they hoped they were not as bad as they had heard. Most had been sent to Black schools, they had not chosen them. Black schools were a place where one wound up, not a place one sought out.

This chapter uses Black schools as a case to further develop the argument that color blind multiculturalism concentrated the stigma of racial/ethnic difference within the category of race. It argues that teachers viewed Black schools through the lens of stigma and tracks the way teachers managed that stigma. Many teachers believed that society stigmatized Black schools as embodying the worst aspects of racial difference. This chapter shows how concentrated stigma, a by-product of hyper-segregation, was only intensified by color blind multiculturalism.

Teachers' stigmatization of Black schools was the flipside of their valorization of multiracial schools. In that sense, this chapter is also about the consequences of productive diversity. Teachers' shared logic for thinking about minority status belied the fact that the Black schools were on the other side of town from the multiracial schools. Still, teachers at both types of school stigmatized racialized minorities. If teachers only valued diversity to the extent that it benefitted them, it is no wonder that some were reluctant to teach at Black schools. Thus, the logic of productive diversity helped mark Black schools as a space of lack.

DIFFERENCES BENEATH THE SURFACE:
BLACK SCHOOLS IN LAKETOWN

The majority of the schools in the study were predominantly Black (7 out of 11). All of the Black schools were located in Black neighborhoods, reflecting Laketown's pronounced racial segregation. The schools had racial composition in common, with all schools having more than 99% Black students, and most of the schools had poverty in common, with the percent of students from low-income families averaging at about 92% across schools (see Table 1.1). Kipps and Erving drove the average percentage of low-income students down, enrolling 70.2% and 88.4% low-income students, respectively. The fact that these two schools were considered middle class shows how poor the schools in Laketown were overall. Besides demographics, the seven schools shared the stigma associated with being Black schools.

Nevertheless, the stigma against Black schools overlooked all the ways the schools were different. For instance, the schools contradicted the stereotype that Black schools were overcrowded. Erving, Kipps, and Foster had the lowest enrollment of all the schools in the study, while the two multiracial schools had some of the highest enrollments (see Table 1.1). The schools also differed in levels of student achievement. Each school had shown gains in their academic achievement, since that was a criterion for inclusion in the study. Thus, these were neither the lowest nor the highest achieving schools in Laketown, but ones that seemed to be on a positive trajectory. Some schools, such as Martin, had been on that trajectory for a longer time, while others, such as Watts, were just beginning their ascent.

Moreover, the schools differed by neighborhood since Black neighborhoods were no more monolithic than Black schools. Like many cities, Laketown had begun investing in some Black areas to attract the returning White middle class, but continued to neglect other Black neighborhoods in less desirable parts of town. Black schools were buffeted by these changes, with some facing closure as the city gentrified their neighborhood, while others gained new status as jewels in their newly revitalized communities. The changing fortunes of their communities affected teacher perceptions of their schools. For some teachers, the uncertain future of their schools made the stigma surrounding Black schools seem even more burdensome. Yet, others had more reason to be hopeful as the star of their school rose with that of the neighborhood.

THE SYMBOLIC BURDEN OF TEACHING AT BLACK SCHOOLS

Teachers at Black schools contended with the negativity with which Black schools were viewed by the rest of society. I term this the symbolic burden of teaching at Black schools, defined as the pervasive social belief that Black schools were undesirable places to teach. Specifically, social opinion conceived of Black schools as being marked by negative characteristics such as disorganization, violence, and academic failure. The symbolic burden of Black schools inverts Fordham and Ogbu's (1986) concept of the burden of "acting White" by examining the stigma attached to Blacks due to expected failure instead of the burden of unexpected success. The burden refers to the constellation of negative meanings surrounding Black ability, achievement, behavior, character, etc.

True to their stigmatizing nature, stereotypes about Blackness were not confined to students, but instead contaminated the entire school and threatened to brand its faculty as dysfunctional and inferior (Goffman, 1986). As a result, managing the stigma took on great urgency as teachers felt personally implicated in criticisms the public lodged with Black schools. Teachers took the negative stereotypes about Black schools into consideration no matter the conditions at their particular school. This symbolic burden was in the background of teachers' talk about Black schools.

Teachers expressed the symbolic burden when they recounted the opinions society held of Black schools. They used what I termed "the chorus" in Chapter 3 as a mouthpiece to express the stigma against Black schools. These absent others stood in for teacher perceptions of social norms in general, that is, as examples of the racial commonsense. However, unlike the teachers at multiracial schools, teachers expected the racial commonsense about Black schools to be negative.

An example from Kipps illustrates the negativity with which teachers expected society to view Black schools. When asked her opinion of the students at Kipps, this White teacher leader said, "I think that I came here with the notion that this was an inner-city school and it was going to be really rough. And it's not." Though she changed her opinion of Black schools through teaching at one, she invoked the common sense toward Black schools by citing her mother's reaction to her coming to Kipps. She continued:

> My mother still has this impression that all our kids bring guns to school. You know? Because I teach in Laketown in the inner city and I'm going to get shot. And maybe I did kind of come in thinking that might be the case, but I guess I'm stupid enough that I came anyway.

Her mother expected Black schools to be violent and the teacher did not blame her as she expected the same thing. According to the teacher, society would consider her "stupid" for teaching at a Black school given the negative characteristics it associated with them. In other words, the teacher believed that society viewed her as abnormal for choosing to teach at a Black school.

The Black principal at Noel described his impression of what society thought of Black schools. Before he arrived, his own teachers believed that Black "kids are dumb." They felt that "we shouldn't expect anything but we should get paid." Moreover, he believed that this view was common to the school system, not just his teachers. He opined, "And I'm sure it wasn't just Noel. I mean it's the school system. That was how teachers felt." Even worse, if teachers did not already feel this way, they were socialized into these negative perceptions. When the interviewer asked, "And so what happened to an energetic teacher who would come in to this school?" The principal replied: "They would generally get a, have to fit in to that type of view. . . . Because that was, that definitely was the overall culture."

The cloud of negative opinion which hung over Black schools meant that teachers were always answering invisible critics; that is the "burden" part of symbolic burden. As a result, many teachers' comments were dedicated to managing the stigma of Black schools. One effect of this burden was that it made some teachers more focused on student deficits than they might have been. These teachers wanted to amass enough evidence to show that someone besides them was responsible for Black school failure. For instance, a Black 2nd grade teacher at Foster complained about the "negative impression" society had of Black schools. She said:

> These people are always telling you what you're not doing and you're terrible at this, and you're terrible at that. That's how we feel as a teacher. But yet people don't understand what it is that we're dealing with, what the challenges are in this environment.

This teacher managed the symbolic burden by suggesting that her interlocutors did not understand what she was up against, indirectly implicating her students and exculpating herself.

Teachers also managed the symbolic burden of the stigma by being provisional about their positive perceptions of Black schools. They constructed Black schools as being either better than expected and thus not good in any absolute way, or exceptionally good, implying that the category of Black schools was still bad. In sum, while public opinion that diversity was valuable worked in favor of multiracial schools, making teacher perceptions more positive than they might have been, public opinion that Blackness was a space of lack drove teacher perceptions down at Black schools.

"A TOUGH PLACE TO HAVE STARTED":
FIRST EXPERIENCES TEACHING AT BLACK SCHOOLS

Given their negative reputation, Black schools did not attract teachers the way multiracial schools did. Teachers were not drawn to Black schools because of their racial composition. Instead, most teachers were placed in Black schools as one of their first teaching assignments. On the face of it, this fact was not entirely surprising, since more Laketown Public Schools (LPS) were single-race, either Black or Latino, rather than multiracial. For example, in 1998 only 10.1% of students in LPS were White, while 53.2% were Black, and 33.4% were Latino (Chicago Public Schools, 2000). This increased the likelihood that teachers would have been assigned to a Black school rather than seeking out one. Still, the lukewarm to negative terms with which teachers described their first experiences with Black schools revealed the low opinion they had of them.

A common theme of teacher stories of coming to teach at Black schools were that they taught "the worst of the worst." Many teachers began their careers at Black schools. Not only did they perceive these first schools as bad, they often described the particular class they had as worse than even the school's norm. This pattern fits with previous research, which found that new teachers at minority schools had more negative perceptions than new teachers at schools that were mostly White (Freeman et al., 1999).

For instance, when a White counselor at Dodge was asked how he entered into education, he replied:

> I don't know, I had always sort of wanted to be an English teacher and actually after doing it a year I never did it again. I taught on the south side of Laketown at Hill High School and it was really tough. They gave me the lowest level functioning freshmen students and I was a kid from Ohio as you know and I went to undergrad school in the corn fields and I had never seen anything like that before, even growing up in Cleveland.

This teacher had such a bad experience teaching at a Black school that he decided to stop teaching English. He implicitly racialized his experience at his first school by contrasting it with the "corn fields," code for the Whiteness, of his undergraduate school. Notice that the teacher said that he taught the lowest students, a sentiment that was repeated in the next interview. Here a Black 5th grade teacher at Brantley reported:

> I came to Brantley and I had lowest, lowest, lowest, lowest of the kids that were readers. And it was really discouraging to me because I come from the

school on the west side and I had a higher level of students for a couple of years and I kind of became accustomed to that.

While this teacher had better experiences at another presumably Black school (given that it was on the west side of Laketown), she started off at Brantley teaching students who were well below her standards. Similarly, a White 3rd grade teacher at Bowen recalled that when she could not get a job there initially, she took job at an after-school program on the south side of Laketown. She said, "I had to basically train the other teachers and then teach the hardest kids of the group which was very hard because they all were really hard." Once again, we get a picture of Black schools as being full of especially difficult students. Finally, a Black 2nd grade teacher at Foster seemed to speak for many teachers whose first teaching experiences were at Black schools when she said, "It's a tough place to have started."

Teachers even suggested that they were lucky to have survived their experiences at the first Black schools where they taught. For instance, when the Black assistant principal at Brantley recounted her first teaching experience at a Black school, she said she entered a school where:

> The Whites were fleeing and Blacks were moving in, in record numbers, and I went to the school and there were only two other Black teachers that were in the school, and those teachers were not used to the Black children that were coming into the school when they came to the school with their own set of problems. I was brand new, I had a class of 55 students, grade 5th and 6th, not one single book because of the growth of the school and they were not prepared for that many children.

After that tumultuous experience, she "knew [she] could make it once [she] taught those fifty-five students, [she] was satisfied being a plain old elementary school teacher." Her comments suggested that she had been through a trial that would equip her for any other school. After her experience at her first Black school, she would be happy to be just a "plain old elementary school teacher." The difficulty of her first school set it apart from the norm.

THE HEART OF DARKNESS:
THE CONCENTRATED STIGMA OF BLACK SCHOOLS

The title "Black school" symbolized more than the race of students in teachers' minds. Teachers envisioned schools where both the teachers and the students were predominantly Black. The faculty at the Black schools in the study were in fact predominantly Black, if we can take demographics of the 2nd and 5th grades as a guide (see Table 1.2). The unmitigated Blackness of Black schools, due to the Blackness of their students, teachers, and neighborhoods, intensified their stigma and gave them an abject status. This concentrated stigma rendered Black schools alienating spaces to many White teachers.

The persistent segregation of American cities like Laketown could only exacerbate the stigma of Black schools. When asked about their backgrounds, several White teachers said that they were from other states or, if they were from Laketown, were from neighborhoods that were unlike the ones in which they taught. Recall, for instance, how alien the students seemed to the teacher who went to undergraduate school in the "corn fields." Likewise, an interviewer reported that a White special education teacher had "(grown) up in Laketown" and "attended the Laketown public schools although it was in another community, which like the community at Watts was low income, but was 'highly integrated.'"

Despite the similarity in community, however, "The classes at her school were larger than at Watts but there were fewer problems because 'society taught the children respect for education system and facilities. If you misbehaved, you could be dealt with,'" she explained. Thus, even with all she had in common with them, this teacher still felt estranged from students at her Black school. For many White teachers, entering Black schools was like entering the fictive "heart of darkness": unruly and slightly hostile spaces in which they were permanent outsiders.

Several White teachers felt like interlopers at Black schools. A White 5th-grade teacher leader at Brantley remembered how the other teachers made her feel like she did not belong when she first got there. She recalled that, "When I first came here they asked me 'Why the hell are you here?' that was the first thing they came in my classroom and asked me and I was subbing." She thought her race, not her status as a substitute teacher, was the cause of their incredulity. When the interviewer asked, "Why did they ask you that?" she replied:

> I don't know. There weren't a lot of Caucasian people in the building I think they felt I was just in here, I mean the Board even asked why they put me in a northwest-side school, they looked at me. That's all they did they looked at me. Lord have mercy. You can look at me but what you see isn't all that you get, there's a lot more than just what you see.

She was upset, but not surprised, that her future co-workers were unwelcoming, given that even the school board questioned her placement at a Black school. Implicitly, she criticized racialized assumptions by saying that "there's a lot more" to her than her race ("what you see.")

At times, school administration had a more active role in sustaining the segregation of the LPS and perpetuating Black schools as Black spaces. A White 6th-grade teacher at Martin almost did not make it there. First, he was "warned off" by friends at another job from taking a school assignment on "the west side" (a Black area). After that, the principal at an all-White school "asked him to come in as a sub 'with no questions asked.'" The interviewer reported that the principal hoped:

> to get [Mr. Smith], a White teacher in an all-White school, assigned as a permanent sub, apparently in violation of the district quota policies concerning the racial balance of teachers in buildings.

Clearly, the Blackness of some Black schools was not an accident, but the result of deliberate actions by administrators. This teacher ended up applying to Martin and liking it, but other White teachers may have been driven or steered away from Black schools by these types of tactics.

White teachers' outsider status estranged them from both their students and their colleagues. As in other research, several White teachers reported feeling abandoned by their Black colleagues, with some Black teachers literally turning their back on them as they struggled with difficult students (Mueller & Price, 1999). The teacher who was almost steered away from Black schools said that other teachers did not talk to him during his first years at Martin for fear that he would not last. He came to the school with a cohort of other White teachers, one of whom was gone by the end of the first month of the school year. This short-lived teacher had "announced his intentions to 'bond with the kids' and [the teacher] saw several of his 6th-grade students hitting the new teacher upside the head in the hallway a week later." The interviewer reported that, "[Mr. Smith] found that the veteran colleagues on the staff would not take much time to get to know him initially," which the interviewer likened to "the Vietnam veteran mentality of not getting to know the new troops well for fear that they might soon be gone."

The teacher leader who first worked as a substitute at Brantley had a similar experience where the teachers at her school did not get to know her initially. She told of an incident from her time as a substitute at the school where her colleagues' every-person-for-themselves attitude could have had disastrous consequences. She said:

> The first week I had a girl . . . She picked up a table in the classroom and I was subbing and she threw it across the room and so I had her in this neck hold, I don't even know what the hold was, and a teacher walked past my room and kept walking. And I saw her later in the hall and I said, "Why did you just keep walking?" and she just walked away from me and I told her I didn't appreciate it and she probably thought, "Who the heck do you think you are?" I don't care; I'm a human being too.

Her colleague's unwillingness to help might have been a test to see if the new teacher was tough enough to make it at Brantley.

Indeed, the incidents at Martin and Brantley reflected a perception across schools that White teachers had trouble controlling their classes. Excerpts from an interviewer's field notes from Watts hinted at this concern.

Ms. Shawn [a Black 5th-grade teacher] explained to me that some of the new students she had received from one of the White teacher's classroom were very disruptive. She explained that, although Mr. Dawson [the White teacher] was a good teacher, especially in science, he was very lax when it comes to discipline and so the students were taking time to adjust to the new environment which requires them to be orderly [in Ms. Shawn's room].

This excerpt suggests that some Black teachers did not expect White teachers to be effective in Black schools, which might help explain their unfriendliness to White teachers.

Other White teachers were made to feel like outsiders by the students. A White teacher, who is now at Bowen, initially found teaching at her previous school, which was predominantly Black, difficult but rewarding until a racist incident drove her away. She recalled that in her "last year there I had kids in my room that [told her], 'My grandmother said, I don't need to listen to you' and this kind of 'you White honkey' and all kinds of things. And I thought, 'you know, I don't need this.'"

Racial tension was not always the source of the distance White teachers felt from Black students, however. Sometimes, White teachers' unfamiliarity with Black interaction styles proved to be a barrier. A White 3rd-grade teacher at Watts suggested as much, when he recalled his first experiences at the school. He said, "I think one of the first few things that struck me . . . was just the extraordinary boldness of the students." His students' interaction style:

can be both a good thing and a bad thing I think. If you can channel them into some sort of positive direction, they're much more apt to tackle tougher issues and go after more deeper knowledge. If you can direct them properly. The problem is that, I've found that they're, it's been difficult to direct. And you're building a lot of firewalls just within the classroom to help direct them in positive directions.

The hyper-segregation of Laketown made it likely that the teacher had not had previous interactions with Black children. In fact, the teacher had done his student teaching at a school he described as "almost like a suburban enclave" within the Laketown Public Schools, which had not prepared him for teaching at Watts.

COPING WITH THE BURDEN OF TEACHING BLACK

Teachers managed the stigma of teaching at Black schools by either clumping or splitting students. They clumped their students in with the average American student by claiming their students were no different than any other. I called this the "kids are just kids" strategy because teachers repeated variations of this phrase across Black schools. Another tactic was for teachers to split their school off from Black schools as a category and single it out as being exceptionally good. Both of these strategies alleviated the stigma attached to a particular school in the short term, but left the status of Black schools as a category unchanged.

Exceptionally Good

Some teachers elevated the status of Black schools by saying they were better than they expected. These teachers lauded Black schools for being exceptions to the rule that Black schools were bad. Often, teachers' comments provided subtle clues that they felt that Black schools were generally not good places to teach. For instance, a White teacher leader at Kipps told the interviewer that she "Chose this school based on . . . the size of the school, the reputation of the school being a nice, good inner-city school with a small population of students." While this teacher praised her particular school, if we look closely at her comments, we see that she is withholding praise for the larger category of inner-city schools. She chose Kipps precisely because of its "reputation" for being different from other inner-city schools, which presumably were not "nice" or "good." Her invocation of the school's reputation suggests that the symbolic burden of Black schools was at play in her decision to choose Kipps. Social opinion went against most Black schools, but Kipps was an exception.

Similarly, another White teacher leader at Kipps believed the school was better than other Black schools and elevated the status of her school as a result. She asserted that she had "learned" from her thirty-plus years teaching that "the kids don't change." Yet, she followed that statement by saying how exceptionally good Kipps was, contradicting her claim that students were of similar quality. When the interviewer asked if she thought the students were "pretty much the same," she replied:

> Yeah, I've always taught on the west side. This is probably the best neighborhood I've taught in. The population is high achieving. I was at Samuel Squire for twenty years. This is special.

Thus, this teacher goes from asserting consistency in the quality of students she has taught at different Black schools to singling Kipps out for being a "special" school with a "high-achieving" population. This subsequent statement gave the impression that good Black schools were rare, even while she seemed to claim that all Black schools were of equal quality.

The next two examples illustrate how low teacher expectations of Black schools could be. Yet, the examples also show the depth of positive teacher perceptions, once their low expectations were proven wrong. A Black 5th-grade teacher at Erving described how she came to teach at that school. Her description shows that she had low expectations of Erving before coming there. In fact, she only visited the school because its principal wore her down with her calls asking her to visit. She reported:

> I had no intentions of transferring to this school because I lived in the south suburbs. And Mrs. Rogers and Dr. Jackson, whom I had never met, kept calling me at home, leaving these messages, "Come over to the school."

Her need to be cajoled into visiting the school is very different from the experience recounted by the teachers who sought out multiracial schools. She was not interested in Erving because it was far from where she lived. However, once she drove through the neighborhood in which the school was located, she had another reason to not want to transfer. She said:

> And I tell people this story all the time. I said, "I'm driving down twelfth street and I'm going, 'Harriet Rogers has lost her mind if she thinks I'm coming over in this neighborhood to work.'"

Thus, the teacher was even more set against transferring once she saw how dysfunctional the neighborhood was. However, something happened when she came into the school that immediately changed her mind. She explained, "I came into the building and you could just feel the difference." She continued:

> And I could just, I could just feel it. And when I met the kids, I didn't meet the kids as I went through the building. Among the children I'm going, "There's really something going on here." And by the time I left [laughs] I had signed transfer of papers.

What happened here? This teacher had little interest in transferring before she visited Erving and was further turned off on the drive over. Yet, once she saw the seriousness of purpose at the school, she signed the transfer papers on the spot. What prompted this sudden reversal of opinion? This teacher's strong positive reaction to Erving might be explained by the depth of her low opinion of the school before coming to visit. She was moved to sign on immediately because she was surprised to find that Erving was a well-functioning school. This was happy news for Erving, but troubling news for Black schools as a whole, since not all prospective teachers will get a chance to visit a school and have their expectations challenged.

The next example shows a similar reversal of opinion that occurred at Watts when a teacher's low expectations were challenged. In this case, a Black 3rd-grade teacher explained to the interviewer how she came to have higher expectations of her own students' academic abilities. The key to her improved perception was the chance to see students succeed at another Black school.

Martin, locally renowned as one of the most successful elementary schools serving poor Black students in the city, was a partner school to Watts, which was on academic probation. As part of that partnership, teachers at Watts observed classes at Martin to get tips on how to improve teaching at their school. Before observing there, this teacher was skeptical of Martin's success:

> At first I thought they said, "Well these kids, my kids can write three paragraphs." And they'd tell us all that and I'm saying, "No they can't." And I was under that impression and I told Dr. Brown I said, "Hey, I don't know what else to do. They're not gonna get that."

The teacher's deeply held belief about the low quality of Black schools was likely the result of the symbolic burden of Black schools. She thought that if her school was low achieving, other Black schools must be as well. Thus, she seemed to believe that Black schools as a category were low achieving. Instead of being open to learning what was making Martin so successful, she initially believed that her students were "not gonna get that."

However, her perceptions changed once she observed classes at Martin. She realized that success was possible at her school because it had happened at Martin. Instead of it being impossible to boost achievement at Watts, her school just needed time to implement some of the practices they used at Martin. She reported:

> And then we went over there, and we were there, and I sit there and it dawned on me, this is just starting in September. So, okay, this is what possibly can happen with us [in] a year at Watts. But we're too far, we're not there yet. Because we just started.

Thus, this 3rd-grade teacher improved her opinion of what was possible at her own school once she encountered a Black school that surpassed her expectations. Her earlier comments suggested that the teacher's negative perceptions of Black schools were entrenched. Her deep-rooted negative perceptions even made her skeptical of the success of a school that was widely hailed for being successful. However, her skepticism turned into fledgling hope that achievement was possible at her school, once she saw Martin's success for herself. Still, Martin remained exceptionally good in her account and exemplified what her school might achieve given time.

Kids Are Just Kids

Another way of managing the stigma against Black schools was for teachers to claim that their schools were no worse than average. Given their stigmatization, even perceiving Black schools as equal to other schools was to elevate their status. The watchword at multiracial schools was "diverse," which teachers typically said with admiration. In contrast, the catchphrase at Black schools was that "kids are just kids." Teachers repeated that mantra across schools when asserting how much the students had in common with the average student, contradicting the perception that Black students were irredeemably "other" and inferior.

A common expression of the "kids are kids" theme was the claim that students needed similar things to do their best: affection, encouragement, and support. This was the conclusion the Black assistant principal at Brantley came to when she said, "I have learned that whether I come from this side of town or this side the children are all the same and they all need the same thing, there is no difference; they need time and affection and if you give them that they will be fine." Similarly, a White teacher leader at Kipps said, "I find that our kids are just kids. You know? They like the same things that other kids do. They have the same securities and insecurities that other children do."

Teachers' comparisons between their students and their real or imagined counterparts at other schools focused on how average their students were, not how good. Thus, one of the most frequent equivalences that teachers drew between their schools and others was that all schools had problems. Because the belief that Black schools were bad was fueled by a racial commonsense, these comparisons had racial implications even when teachers did not explicitly use racial discourse in their comments.

For instance, a 5th-grade Black teacher leader at Brantley said that attending a workshop allowed her to see that other schools had similar problems as hers. She said of one particularly good workshop:

And that was one of the best nights that I spent at that school. Because there were teachers there, and so sitting down with other teachers and being able to say, "Okay, I'm not the only one who has this major headache when I leave work." Because . . . it was teachers from all around the city.

This allowed her to understand:

Even though you're on the north side and you're in the [. . .] that's supposed to be a better school than where I am. You're still having the same problems. They may be a little different but your problems are still the same.

Thus, this teacher was able to see that her school was no worse than average.

Meanwhile, the principal at Kipps said that all schools shared the problem of not having enough resources. When asked to name some of the resources she used in her work as a school leader, she told the interviewer, "You never have enough money to purchase all that you need so that's probably an ongoing kind of thing and not just in this school probably in all schools. You never have enough." Like the previous teacher, this principal was looking over her shoulder to compare her school's resources to other imagined schools.

While the teachers in the previous examples did not explicitly use racial language, other teachers did invoke racial categories when making comparisons between students. These teachers explicitly asserted similarities between racial groups that may typically seem too distinct to compare. Teachers were implicitly drawing on color blind ideology when they asserted that different racial groups were similar to each other. They either argued that group differences did not matter or, alternately, that students should be judged as individuals, not as members of groups. These two positions shared the assumption that racial distinctions were immaterial. Thus, color blindness provided the ideology that made the claim that "kids are just kids" plausible. When overt racism held more sway, teachers might have faced much more resistance to their claim that students of different races, particularly Black and White kids, were similar.

Teachers identified similarities between Blacks and other students of color and between Blacks and Whites. The point of these comparisons was to neutralize the symbolic burden of Black schools by asserting that racial distinctions were exaggerated. Some teachers perceived similarities between Black schools and other minority schools. For instance, a White teacher leader at Brantley said of a math curriculum they wanted to introduce at her school, "And they had said in some of the Latino communities that it was good. Now if it addresses bilingual kids, where there's a whole can of worms there, we might be able to address our kids." Here she implies that both Black and Latino schools face similar challenges in teaching their kids.

Perhaps more telling were the similarities teachers perceived between Black and White schools. For instance, the principal at Brantley recounted that she tried to convince her teachers to use a new literacy program by sending them to observe another school. She said she sent the teachers to, "Stuart school, which is on the northwest side (and) is a different population of children, but children are children." Stuart is a predominantly White school, so the principal was asserting equivalence between Black and White schools. She put racial distinctions into play, in a city as racially segregated as Laketown, by mentioning the location of the school where she sent her teachers to observe. By mentioning the location of the school, the principal signaled her awareness that some might think practices that worked at a White school would not work at a Black school; however, she immediately dismissed this view by saying "children are children."

The White assistant principal at Noel also perceived similarities between Black and White schools. When asked what she thought of the neighborhood where the school was located, she said:

More kids like to come to school than I would've expected when I first came over, because I always heard negative things about the west side. It's not true. It's just like it is in the south side, north side, wherever you go. These kids want to be in school.

This assistant principal also seemed to have racial distinctions in mind, since the south and west sides of Laketown are thought to be Black areas while the north side is imagined to be a White area. Additionally, she invoked the opinion of the absent other, those unnamed people who told her that students at Black schools did not want to learn. In other words, she invoked social opinion. Fortunately, this assistant principal found out that the desire to learn was color blind—students at schools of all different types of racial compositions wanted to learn.

Despite the encroachment of color blind ideology, many teachers still took the differences between Black and White schools for granted. For instance, recall the teacher at Watts who opined that his school was "obviously something completely different" than his former school on the northwest side, which he likened to "a suburban enclave in the city of Laketown." Thus, the principal at Brantley and others who asserted similarities between Black and White schools were challenging a racial commonsense that held that schools were "obviously" different by race. A Black teacher at Martin openly named the distinctions that people made between Black schools and White suburban schools. She spoke of being frustrated when she attended a workshop for a program that she believed would not work at her school. She explained:

> The means of our inner-city children are much different than those of a suburban child. I spoke with a suburban parent . . . there wasn't any need for special needs instructors in the suburbs and I had to remind him "What reason was it for you to move to the suburbs to begin with?" . . . The problems that my children are having are the very ones that you have tried to escape; where you [call it] special education/remediation . . . in your suburban system, it's called special needs here. But it's still needed.

According to the teacher, the parent clung to the belief that suburban schools did not need programs like special education, only Black schools did. In fact, she accused the parent of leaving the city to escape the problems she associated with Black schools. In that climate where teachers expected others to perceive Black schools as being different and worse than White schools, the principal's assertion at Brantley that her kids and the kids from a northwest side school could learn from the same literacy program was radical.

At first glance, the two strategies for coping with the burden of teaching at Black schools, declaring Black students to be as good as average and claiming that one's school was exceptionally good, seemed contradictory. The "kids are just kids" tactic placed Black students within the norm, while the exceptionally good strategy said that they exceeded the norm. Yet, these divergent strategies had similar advantages and disadvantages. On one hand, claims to be exceptionally good or no worse than average were both improvements on the general perception that Black schools were bad. The benefit of saying one's school was exceptionally good is obvious, but the utility of claiming to be average may be less so. In a climate that placed Black students below the norm, claiming that Black students were like any other raised their status. Thus, both strategies could neutralize the stigma attached to Black schools.

Yet, both strategies had the same limitation of overlooking the strengths of Black schools as a category. For instance, teachers could have cast Black students' ability to make progress in the face of multiple disadvantages as a special strength of Black schools. The inability to perceive strengths in Black schools as a whole contrasted with the virtues teachers attributed to multiracial schools as a category. Teachers posited some Black schools as exceptions to the rule and offered others as proof that Black schools were within the norm. However, the center still held: Black schools as a category were rarely recognized for their unique strengths.

RESPONDING TO THE UNIQUE NEEDS OF BLACK SCHOOLS

At multiracial schools, teachers were eager to describe the benefits they gained from teaching there. Specifically, they welcomed the chance to teach about tolerance, learn about the other, and prove that pluralism worked. Most teachers at multiracial schools felt personally and professionally enriched by their experience.

In contrast, teachers felt challenged, not enriched, by their experience at Black schools. Yet, they were matter–of–fact about the accommodations they made for student differences and deficits. This pragmatism was significant, since other schools in Laketown, especially those labeled as failing, may have responded to deficits by giving up on students. Still, teachers were more likely to talk about what they had to settle for or accommodate rather than what they gained from teaching at Black schools.

A common concession was that teachers adjusted their teaching to make up for students' lack of basic skills. Sometimes teachers addressed these deficits indirectly by using culturally relevant pedagogy that shored up students' self-esteem and raised their racial awareness. Teachers did not frame all differences as deficits, however. For instance, some teachers believed that Black students needed particular styles of discipline. They saw these adjustments as responses to demographics, rather than concessions to deficits.

Making Up for Basic Skills

Teachers at Black schools often noted that their students lacked basic academic skills, particularly literacy. Some students were very behind, such as in a school described below, where 7th and 8th graders could not read and write. Though many teachers at Black schools expected students to be behind, most did not give up on their students. Instead, they adjusted their teaching practices to make up for what their students lacked. They were pragmatic, but not fatalistic, about students' deficits.

The Black assistant principal at Bowen illustrated this matter-of-fact approach to student deficits at her previous school. A Laketown native, she returned to her former elementary school as a classroom teacher upon finishing her undergraduate degree. However, the extent of illiteracy at her alma mater alarmed her enough to get graduate training as a reading specialist. She explained that her colleagues misunderstood their students' problems:

> They thought they had a lot of discipline problems. These kids had all kinds of labels because they could not read. But what it was, some of them had never been taught how to read. They were just given a book and some questions, asked to read, answer the questions, and that's where the frustration begins.

Her solution was to get to the root of her students' apparent "discipline problems," their inability to read. Her success baffled some of her colleagues who could not see past the students' deficits.

> So when I got a class that was really low and teachers and other people noticed that they were able to, they weren't having the discipline problems that maybe they had had the year prior, they wondered what was the secret. There was no secret. It's just that these kids were frustrated because they were being put on the spot to try to read and being embarrassed because they couldn't read and I'm talking like 7th and 8th grade kids here who should have had some . . . phonics and vocabulary that was never put on the Iowa Tests. They were scoring two and three years below their reading levels.

This assistant principal could address the cause of students' problems, their illiteracy, because she took its symptom, their behavior problems, in stride.

Similarly, a Black 5th-grade teacher Brantley was realistic about her students' lack of basic skills, but did not give up on them because of it. Instead, she decided to build on what her students could do instead of focusing on what they could not do. She "really worked on" developing strategies that increased their comprehension:

> And I noticed a big difference last year when I was able to bring in different ways of being able to teach kids who may not be as good readers, but can read something and still have a comprehension, they comprehend it but expressing it, they don't express it the same way. And sometimes they do it, express it in

pictures or they really can express it in pictures, or using magazine pictures to
retell a story. It's just all different strategies to get them to try to understand.

The teacher made progress by meeting her students where they were.

Meanwhile, a White 6th-grade teacher at Martin developed ingenious ways
to address his students' lack of basic math skills. According to the interviewer, this
included:

Teaching methods such as giving out candy for students who would do well
and encouraging his students to get involved in learning activities in his
classroom instead of sitting in their desks in rows.

Though his colleagues were skeptical about his methods:

An end-of-the-year assembly to honor Iowa Test results showed that student
after student in his class came forward to accept progress awards, then
honored [the teacher] as an outstanding math teacher.

While his methods were unusual, they were proactive responses to student deficits,
as were the responses by the teachers at Brantley and Bowen.

Teachers at both multiracial and Black schools had to adjust their teaching in response to school demographics. Where teachers at multiracial schools
enjoyed the challenge of making their teaching multicultural, teachers at Black
schools found nothing to celebrate about their students' lack of basic skills. Still,
many teachers had pragmatic responses to student deficits across Black schools.
Thus, while student demographics did not inspire professional excitement at Black
schools as they did at multiracial schools, they did foster creative teaching.

Creating a Race-Conscious Environment

Black schools differed from multiracial schools in their emphasis on improving basic skills. As we have seen, teachers adjusted their pedagogy to accommodate students' deficits. Black schools also tailored their environment to fit their
students in other ways. These adjustments were not accommodations to deficits,
but rather acknowledgments of how race affected the learning environment. Specifically, teachers believed that Black students were best served when they had a
curriculum and a style of discipline that reflected the student body. In this way,
Black schools strove to create a race-conscious environment.

Black schools engaged in many practices that could be seen as culturally relevant pedagogy. Culturally relevant pedagogy builds on students' racial and ethnic
background and incorporates their experiences, perspectives, and learning styles to
help empower them in school and society (Gay, 2000). A key way Black schools

created a race-conscious environment was to have curriculum and activities that featured Blacks. This meant that Black history was taught year-round and gave Black History Month a high profile at Black schools. For instance, a Black 2nd-grade teacher at Watts reported that the celebration at her school included not only a "Black history assembly," but also "an African-American festival" that involved vendors from the community.

The Black principal at Kipps described the various ways her school infused her school with Black history:

> We teach them about their heritage from the moment they step in the building which is evident with our morning opening in which we do the National Anthem, we also do the Black National Anthem, "Lift Ev'ry Voice," and we have a thought for today and we also have a quiz daily, a trivia kind of question based upon Black history in which children—we do it over the PA and they ring the office if they have the answer.

She thought these efforts were necessary to "help build self-esteem," saying "They need to hear how Blacks contribute to the growth of this country in every aspect of it and that's what we want them to know."

Teachers at multiracial schools also celebrated their students' heritage, but their aim was to foster tolerance among students and educate themselves about other cultures. In contrast, teachers at Black schools tied teaching Black History to increasing Black students' power. Kipps was unique among Black schools in that it had a Black History teacher. When asked to explain the mandate for her class, she told the interviewer she had "free reign" as long as she covered the required history curriculum. This flexibility meant that she could "get away from" the "teacher's edition" as soon as she was able and teach issues about which she felt "passionate." For instance, she brought in the newspaper so that her students could discuss a racially motivated fight that had happened in the city. She confessed:

> Sometimes if I feel kind of controversial, I ask, "How do you feel about that, do you feel they're being treated unfairly because of their race?" Sometimes, I take my fights out in the classroom.

She was teaching students to think critically about how racial inequality shaped their world. Far from merely taking out her fights in the classroom, this teacher was fulfilling culturally relevant pedagogy's mandate to challenge the status quo.

The drive to teach Black students about inequality was not limited to specialized teachers. At Foster, a White 2nd-grade teacher sought to make her students "lifelong learners" because she wanted to empower them. She explained:

So I think that just as important as getting down those basic skills is children need to be empowered through literacy and through communication and through experiences to go further and to take what they've learned further to do something to improve not only their lives, but the lives around them.

She empowered her students to positively affect their environment by "providing a very print-rich environment" where the newest books were always on the shelf. However, another way to empower them was:

To have class discussions that are very much focused on the children's lives and their futures and to never forget their history, the struggles and the successes of their history, and to constantly have that shaping their learning and their own interests, too.

Thus, while teachers did not claim culturally relevant pedagogy as an influence on their teaching, they were nonetheless following its mandate of teaching to encourage social responsibility.

Black Discipline

Teachers also adjusted their discipline styles based on their beliefs about what African-American students needed. For instance, the principal at Kipps believed that schools discouraged Black students from "expressing themselves." She said:

. . . I think our children are not allowed, African-American children, are not allowed to express ourselves the way that we should. Because for too long we sort of talk at our children, not to them, and we discourage. A lot of verbalization, a lot of it we discourage. So I'd like for the school to be a haven where you can kind of develop those kinds of things and that helps them to be confident about themselves.

Where the principal at Kipps was worried that Black students were not given enough freedom, several teachers thought Black students needed a firm hand to control their behavior. For instance, a teacher at Watts said that she believed "in strict discipline." She elaborated:

I believe in "get that behind," yes, I do. And that's one of the things that we've lost. And I think it's so tragic because our children have missed what discipline, what respect is. And they don't have any respect for education because they've missed it. They don't have any respect for authority because this society says you can't, you can't spank your children.

The teacher used the possessive "our children," making it unclear as to whether she was talking about the needs of her students at Watts or of Black students in general. Yet, the tone of unspoken understanding she struck with the interviewer, who was also Black, suggested that she believed that Black students generally needed unique types of discipline. She acknowledged that corporal punishment was out of favor with mainstream educators who would prefer her to use "psychology" on students. She disagreed, saying:

Teacher: I've got some psychology for them.
Interviewer: Yeah, yeah.
Teacher: It is called the belt. And most of my parents tell me, "Ms. Evelyn, take care of your business."
Interviewer: Go ahead.
Teacher: Handle your business. You know what? My students know. Ms. Evelyn will handle her business. Okay? Not abusive, Dr. Jordan, not abusive at all.

The teacher argued that while her authoritative style may have been out of step with mainstream educators, it met the expectations of her audience, Black parents. However, the pull of mainstream norms was powerful. We can see this in the teacher's insistence that her use of spanking was "not abusive." Ms. Evelyn clearly was not responding to Dr. Jordan's criticism of spanking, given his agreement with her statements. Instead, she seemed to be anticipating the way that those outside of her school might misinterpret her actions and label her behavior.

In another instance, a Black 2nd-grade teacher at Martin recalled that she felt ill-suited to teach at the White suburban school she observed as a student teacher. She believed that her disciplining style would better match the needs at a Black school. The interviewer reported that:

She concluded that she wouldn't be able to teach students at a predominantly White, affluent school because parents there are overly concerned about the rights of students. She commented on how some teachers' teaching style and classroom management styles in such schools are frequently challenged by parents as perhaps being too aggressive or too strict. She said in Black schools it doesn't work that way. Sometimes being aggressive is precisely what the students need. Sometimes being forceful with kids who come from the unstable kinds of homes that her students come from is exactly what they need and respond to. She prefers to be in an environment where her style is consistent with how her students' parents discipline their own children.

In an inversion of the usual hierarchy, this Black teacher preferred poor Black schools over affluent White schools. Like the teacher from Watts, she believed that Black schools required a distinctive style of discipline that she was equipped to provide.

Black schools were not unique in their attempt to create an environment that was responsive to students' difference. Multiracial schools were also sensitive to their students' difference, primarily their ethnic heritage. Thus, where multiracial schools held Multicultural Days, Black schools held African-American Festivals. However, teachers at multiracial schools were distinct in their belief that they gained from learning about their students' background. Chapter 3 showed that teachers felt personally enriched by what they learned about their students' heritage, since multiculturalism had given knowledge about foreign cultures social value.

Teachers related very differently to the task of incorporating Black culture into Black schools. For the most part, teachers at Black schools described how creating a race conscious environment benefitted their students, not how it benefitted them. This was likely due to a few factors. For one thing, racial mismatch between students and teachers was not as pronounced at Black schools as at multiracial schools. Unlike the predominantly White faculty at multiracial schools, Black teachers were already familiar with Black culture, which eliminated the "learning about the other" appeal of creating a racially conscious environment.

Yet, another factor was that multiculturalism did not have the same effect on knowledge of Black culture as it did on knowledge of White ethnic and Asian culture. Multiculturalism raised the status of knowledge of foreign groups, not knowledge of native-born minorities. Thus, White teachers at Black schools did not express excitement about learning about Black culture, even though much of it may have been foreign to them. At the same time, Black teachers rarely said they felt rewarded by teaching about Black culture, notwithstanding exceptions such as the teacher at Kipps who felt she was fighting her battles in the classroom. The racial difference of Black schools did not make them more desirable to teachers, as did the composition of multicultural schools, but it obligated them to respond to that difference.

ADRIFT IN THE AMERICAN DREAM:
HOW DIVERSITY LEFT BLACK SCHOOLS BEHIND

Color blind multiculturalism placed Blacks outside the bounds of the dominant American narrative of difference. Diversity discourse had to do with celebrating ethnic difference. This conception of ethnicity featured the narrative of the triumphant immigrant, who overcame obstacles that he or she encountered in the New World. The triumph of the immigrant is central to the narrative; it is what gives ethnicity the power to rehabilitate America's claim to being a democratic nation (Hsu, 1996). The immigrant story becomes *the* American story when immigrants prove that ethnic difference did not stop them from achieving mobility (Hsu, 1996). In this way, immigrant minorities could embody the American Dream.

Color blind multiculturalism gave new meaning to multiracial schools. Multiculturalism put ethnic difference in a new light; instead of a burden it became a source of pride. At the same time, color blindness brought on an ethnic turn, the propensity to see difference in terms of ethnicity rather than race. Teachers turned from racial thinking and its uncomfortable associations with inequality to ethnicity and its capacity to rehabilitate America's history of discrimination.

Framed this way, diversity discourse did not elevate the status of Blacks. Instead, it concentrated the stigma associated with minority status into the category of race as opposed to ethnicity. Color blind multiculturalism separated immigrant minorities out from native-born minorities, especially Blacks, leaving the disadvantages of minority status to pool at the bottom of the status hierarchy. It glued Blacks to the bottom of the totem pole by heaping the stigma of being a minority on them without the rehabilitative mantle of ethnicity to alleviate its negativity.

Black schools bore the brunt of this concentrated stigma. While the two multiracial schools I discussed in Chapter 3 had many different types of minority students (including Blacks), they were mainly minorities with the right kind of difference, that is, difference associated with ethnicity. In contrast, the seven Black schools that I discussed in this chapter were overwhelmingly Black. Moreover, the schools had predominantly Black faculty and were located in hyper-segregated Black neighborhoods (see Table 1.2 for teacher demographics). Because of this, teachers perceived Black schools as Black spaces; not just Black in their student body, but in every other important aspect as well. Where the diversity of multiracial schools had currency, the unadulterated Blackness of Black schools only intensified their stigma. In short, Black students represented the wrong kind of difference to many teachers and the overwhelming Blackness of Black schools compounded that perception.

CHAPTER 5

Not Quite White
Preserving the White Norm

A lot of our ethnic groups don't talk to one another, they don't relate to this being the traditional way—I'm gonna generalize here, in the way your average middle-class family does—that it's just natural that you be involved in the PTA or the (school council) type thing, that you volunteer.

—A White parent, chair of the school council at Dodge,
explaining how the diversity of his school affected parent involvement

Despite their celebration of diversity, teachers never treated immigrant minorities as the new normative student. Instead, native-born, White middle-class students remained their touchstone for issues like normal student achievement and behavior and normal parent participation. The previous chapters showed that a shift had occurred that imbued minority status with new value. Nevertheless, teachers continued to invoke the middle class, which they implicitly constructed as White, as the standard by which to judge students and schools. This subtle form of bias meant that schools still advantaged White middle-class students more than immigrant minority students.

The advantages of normativity, while often invisible, are nonetheless real. Because the normal is seen as positive, teachers associated positive things with students they perceived as normative (Perry, 2001). Thus, teachers associated middle-class students with positive characteristics such as high achievement and involved parents. Normativity also implies deviance and constructs difference from the norm as abnormal, rather than as legitimate.

Teachers in the study did label the ways minorities differed from Whites as deviant, for instance, by faulting Black and Latino parents for not following the middle-class pattern of being involved. Yet, the narrative of rehabilitative ethnicity allowed teachers to make further distinctions among minorities that gave immigrant minorities a relative advantage over Blacks. Specifically, teachers moved from labeling students as normal and deviant, to judging who was closer to the standard and judging the legitimacy of their reasons for not meeting the standard. This book has been concerned with exposing these finer levels of distinctions up until this point. However, the goal of this chapter is to return to that first distinction, between normal and deviant, to underline the persistence of Whiteness as the norm.

This chapter describes how the teachers in the study constructed the normative student and identifies privileges associated with normativity. Normativity actually contained multiple qualities of which race was only one component. Teachers constructed the normative student as White, middle-class, native-born, and mainstream. Yet, while normativity contained multiple qualities, teachers tied each factor to Whiteness either explicitly or implicitly in their talk. Most significantly, teachers used a class discourse that was implicitly raced White to describe the normal student. Thus, the word "White" is missing, but implied, in the description of the "average middle-class family" that the parent invoked in the quote that begins this chapter. For that reason, this chapter asserts that Whiteness was central to the construction of normativity.

Thus, teachers perpetuated White normativity while embracing diversity. This third component of assimilating diversity made the other two components possible. Confident in the fact that the White middle class was still normative, teachers were free to appreciate the enriching differences that Latino and Asian students brought. They could engage in productive diversity without fearing that the dominant culture would lose its status. Moreover, the differences that they valued in ethnicized minorities, such as their traditional morality, also put the dominant culture in a good light. Teachers believed that immigrant minorities had values that were similar to their own: They were hard-working, clean, and honest. While assimilating diversity seemed like a big break from America's racist past, it actually gave teachers a way to reconcile White privilege with recognizing difference.

NOT WHITE

The distinctions teachers made between White students gives an interesting slant on White normativity. A significant minority of Laketown's immigrant population was from Europe. At the time of the study, 20% of Laketown residents were immigrants and 26% of those immigrants were from Europe (Garner, 2007). In contrast to earlier generations of European immigrants, but in keeping with the post-1965 wave, many of these immigrants were from Eastern European countries that were formerly ruled by the Soviet Union. Accordingly, 50% of the European immigrants in Laketown were from Poland or Russia (Garner, 2007). Moreover, some of these recent White European immigrants were not immigrants at all, but refugees from the Yugoslavian and Bosnian Wars of the 1990s.

Their religion also distinguished the recent White European immigrants from earlier generations of European immigrants. Some of the refugees from the wars were Muslim, while many of the Russian immigrants were Jewish. Thus, the recent White European immigrants differed in multiple ways from the European immigrants on whom the model of White assimilation is based. They were from

Eastern instead of Western Europe, were Jewish and Muslim instead of Christian, and were sometimes refugees fleeing conflict rather than immigrants searching for better lives.

For these reasons, teachers treated White immigrants as immigrants, not as Whites. For instance, they often listed White immigrant groups as among those that contributed to the positive diversity of their schools. A Black teacher at Stanley, a Latino school, said that she missed the diversity of her former school. She said:

> Teacher: I mean there were just so many different kinds of kids speaking different languages.
>
> Interviewer: Right, right.
>
> Teacher: You know we had kids from Lithuania and just all over Eastern bloc nations. They were in my school.
>
> Interviewer: Wow.
>
> Teacher: And then you had these other kids who were there. So that was really cool.
>
> Interviewer: Must have been a really good experience for all the students there.
>
> Teacher: It was. It was. I mean that's diversity in practice.

That the teacher included European ethnicities as part of the good diversity at her former school showed that she viewed White immigrants as just another valued immigrant population.

Presumably, teachers could value White immigrants as both Whites and immigrants, but in practice teachers rarely spoke of White immigrants in this way. Instead, teachers grouped White immigrants along with immigrants of color, rarely making distinctions between them, and treated Whiteness as something separate. Recall, for instance, how the White teacher at Dodge counted White immigrants as among the immigrant populations that contributed to the language diversity at her school, saying: "The four major languages in the neighborhood are Russian, Assyrian, Burdo, and Spanish, and then there's a multitude of other East European languages, other Asian languages." Here Russian and "other East European languages" are equivalent to and interchangeable with "Burdo" and "Spanish," unremarkable except as foreign languages that reflect the diversity of Dodge's sizeable immigrant population.

The ethnicity and immigrant status of White immigrants are what was salient to the teacher, not their race. Since Whiteness operates through not being bound by an ethnicity, except when Whites opt to identify ethnically, teachers effectively obscure the Whiteness of Russians and other White immigrants when they discuss them in this way (Gallagher, 2003). Teachers made their White immigrants' Whiteness socially unimportant, attending instead to their ethnicity. However, as we will see, Whiteness obscured or downplayed is Whiteness denied.

Teachers also attributed the same characteristics to White immigrants as to immigrant minorities, such as having extended families or traditional values. A Middle Eastern teacher at Dodge offered Yugoslavians as an example of the large, extended families that were typical of immigrants at his school. He said:

> Teacher: Because a lot of the kids are like their brothers they will be coming here next year, it's a large family, you know them all there is probably a hundred families in this school. That's how I feel because they are all related to each other.
> Interviewer: So there are a lot of relatives going to school here together?
> Teacher: Yeah a lot of cousins, I don't know if they *are* cousins, a lot of Yugoslavians will say, "Oh there goes my cousin, he's in room 233" . . . Three sets of cousins. I know that a couple [of the students] are because they all live together.

This teacher distanced Yugoslavian students from the normative White student by describing their families in this way. Teachers perceived extended families as typical of immigrant students, not native-born White students. By constructing White European immigrants as not quite White, teachers denied them the full benefits of White privilege.

NOT AMERICAN

Teachers had a complicated relationship with assimilation and thus American-ness. On the one hand, teachers liked that their White European immigrant and immigrant minority students retained their ethnic difference because they enjoyed their culture. At the same time, many teachers believed that students should eventually assimilate and become American. We saw shades of this when teachers discussed their misgivings about bilingual education. Assimilation ideology also structured teachers' perceptions of the normative student. Specifically, teachers constructed having an American heritage as the basis of normativity, even in schools with large immigrant populations. In other words, though teachers appreciated ethnic diversity, they still considered American culture and heritage the standard.

"American" signified the normal, implicitly White, student. A sign that teachers meant for American to stand for normal and White is that teachers did not use racial and ethnic categories when talking about White American students as they did when discussing White European immigrant and minority students. A Middle Eastern teacher at Dodge used American as implicitly White and normative in this exchange:

Interviewer: It's so diverse.
Teacher: Yes I think I have three kids that are American, maybe even . . . no,
I have three.

He continued by partially enumerating the groups that constituted his school's diversity, saying, "Yeah there are Hispanics, but most are Indian, Pakistani, Syrians, Yugoslavians, and lot of Russian and Mexicans."

We examined this excerpt in Chapter 3, but I want to emphasize different things here. Other scholars have found that individuals restrict American to mean White American, not African American or other native-born minority groups (McBride, 2005). Thus, the teacher probably meant "White" when he said "American." Moreover, he meant *native-born* White since he included "Yugoslavians," and "Russians" as among the students who made the school "diverse." In other words, he excluded White immigrants from American-ness and, by extension, from full Whiteness.

Some teachers were explicit about seeking to assimilate their students. While color blind multiculturalism taught teachers to appreciate foreignness, many teachers ultimately favored Americanization as the goal of education. For instance, while a White teacher at Dodge initially said the challenges his school faced were not different from any other school, he eventually said that his sizeable immigrant student population had unique needs. He said:

Because our first challenge is to teach kids and to get [them] to reach the best results . . . Well, to make them American. . . . To make them feel comfortable in this country and to feel satisfaction . . .

His school's large immigrant population meant his students had different challenges than the typical student. While teachers' celebrations of diversity could have meant that Americanization had fallen out favor, this teacher's comments suggested that it had not. Many teachers saw their students' foreignness as something that they had to rectify.

Teachers noted their students' lack of American-ness in other ways. Some teachers treated American-ness as a storehouse of experiences that they did not share with their White immigrant and immigrant minority students. When the interviewer asked her to explain "why you think it's important for students to learn about the Holocaust at this grade level," a White teacher at Dodge replied:

Any kids or my kids? My kids because most of their parents are not U.S. citizens, they've been through their own troubles but they need to know what worldwide we should look at it as something that was terrible. Some people will say they were in a country that wasn't—didn't have troops fighting in

World War II, whereas, my family, we're 4th- or 5th-generation Americans, so I come from a family where my parents' generation, the war was the biggest thing that happened as far as the change in their life when they were growing and I feel it's something that the kids need to be aware of equally to other things going on in the world.

Notice how the teacher suggested that her kids needed to learn about the Holocaust for different reasons than "any kids." By "any kids" she seemed to mean the average American student.

The teacher placed herself within the narrative of the typical American whose family had been in the United States for generations while explaining why it was important to teach about the Holocaust. She implied that to be a true American was to have memories of how World War II transformed America, not just the recent wars in Eastern Europe and the Middle East. School would help her students catch up with what the typical student already knew about the war from family history. The teacher marked her immigrant students as potentially permanent outsiders, since they could never have the American heritage that she had.

In this way, teachers made the fact that their students were not native-born Americans salient. Teachers noted their students' foreignness in ways that separated immigrant students from the normative student. For instance, a White teacher at Dodge who was a champion of the school's diversity revealed that he did not perceive his students to be fully American. Typical of him, he was excitedly describing an aspect of the school's diversity to the interviewer:

International Bazaar is one of the highlights of the school year. And it's coordinated by the bilingual department. And each nationality is represented down there. And we just represented the U.S. with those two songs. We're the U.S. contingent each year. Although we have, probably out of 21 kids in that guitar group . . . about eight languages, so we're not really U.S., but we're U.S. And it's a terrific thing. It's what the school is all about.

The teacher granted students ethnic credits by celebrating how their presence enriched the school, but also denied their American-ness. The key segment of the quote is when he said the guitar group contained "about eight languages," "so we're not really U.S., but we're U.S." He seemed to be using "eight languages" as a sign that the students were immigrants and implying that immigrant students were "not really" American.

The teacher's comments reflected teachers' complicated relationship with the foreignness of their students. On one hand, the teacher's belief that immigrant students could represent America fit with a common belief that America was a "nation of immigrants" (Jacobson, 2008). Yet, at the same time, the teacher also seemed to be preserving full American-ness for the native-born by saying the guitar group was "not really" American.

A White teacher from Putnam was struggling more obviously with the tension between balancing diversity and assimilation. She launched into a meditation on identity when asked a standard question about her race/ethnicity:

Interviewer: How would you characterize your race/ethnicity?
Teacher: My race?
Interviewer: Um hum.
Teacher: I guess I'm a European White person.
Interviewer: Okay.
Teacher: But American. Like I tell the kids.... You know they send us a racial/ethnic survey. And I understand the reason for it. They want to make sure, and they really have to make sure, that funds are being distributed equitably.
Interviewer: Yeah.
Teacher: And so I'm sitting here and I say, "Hey, you know we're all Americans but, you know, which of you are Puerto Rican?"

A few things are interesting about this teacher's comments. First, she seemed uncomfortable with thinking in racial terms. Her hesitation before answering the question, indicated by her asking the interviewer to repeat it, suggested discomfort with the question, while her statement that she "guessed" that she was a "European White American" suggested embarrassment with applying a racial label to herself. Research shows that Whites are not used to thinking of themselves in racial terms, which might explain the teacher's hesitation (Frankenberg, 1993).

She continued to show discomfort with racial thinking in her ruminations about identity. She seemed to believe that racial labels were divisive and excluded groups from an American identity. Thus, she followed her racial self-identification with "but American." This suspicion of racial categories is common to color blind and assimilationist thinking (Bonilla-Silva, 2003). Color blindness reinforces racial hierarchies by erasing the continuing salience of race. Identifying racially does not have to contradict identifying as an American, but her statement treats them as contradictory identities. Thus, while she seemed to intend inclusion of racial/ethnic minorities when she said "we're all Americans," she perpetuated the color blind notion that to be truly American was to be racially unmarked.

NOT MAINSTREAM

Teachers favored immigrant minorities in part because they believed that they were culturally closer to Whites—in their traditional family form and decency, for instance. Thus, teachers were often reaffirming the value of behavior they coded as White even when they lauded immigrant minorities. Yet, despite their similarities to Whites, teachers perceived immigrant minorities as nonetheless distinct from them. Teachers slotted immigrant minorities in the honorary White category of receiving some status, but not the full range of privileges that Whites enjoy (Bonilla-Silva, 2004).

While teachers lauded Latinos for their family-mindedness, they sometimes took exception with the patriarchal gender roles they perceived in their culture. A Black teacher at Putnam felt she had to become a surrogate "basketball mom" for her kids to make up for what their mothers did not provide. She explained:

> Teacher: Either they don't . . . a lot of our parents don't drive. They don't have that second or third car available to them. A lot of our moms because of their culture that has transferred from Mexico or wherever they're from to America, women are . . . they stay at home.
> Interviewer: Um, right.
> Teacher: And you've got this very strict tradition. The dad has the car and so we have a lot of moms who would like to participate but they can't. Unless it's warm and the field is down the street and they can walk and bring the babies with them.

The teacher believed that patriarchal gender roles based in "culture that has transferred from . . . Mexico or wherever" prevented Latina mothers from attending their children's games. She thought the mothers who "wanted to participate" were prevented from traveling to games due to "strict tradition" that held that "dad has the car." In contrast, her explanation of why Latino fathers were not involved harkened back to the approving narrative of the overworked immigrant. She explained, "Of course a lot of our daddies cannot participate because they're working."

The teacher was more explicit than many others in her construction of mainstream culture. She contrasted the lack of involvement of Latino parents at her current school with the more typical level of involvement of parents at her previous school. These families had "that second or third car . . . available to them," which made it easier for them to attend school games. Thus, middle-class status became a marker of mainstream values. She picked up the class theme later in the interview, saying:

> Teacher: So rarely do you see a family member at a basketball game or something like that. It's just not the case. I think in your more affluent communities that's very prevalent, like where I was.
> Interviewer: Um hum, right, right.
> Teacher: It was very affluent and so even if the moms weren't at home or the dads weren't home they took time off. They would come on lunch. We had a lot of parents who came during their lunchtime to sit with the kids, read stories to the whole group.

Her comments suggested that she did not see the families at her former school as typical, either, because they were "very affluent," not just middle class. Yet, they were closer to the mainstream in the value they placed on participating in school. While most parents may not be in the position to take time off from work to read to their kid's class, parents with more mainstream values were more likely to do so.

Likewise, the White principal at Stanley thought Mexican mothers were not as assertive as their American counterparts. She too believed their circumscribed role had negative effects on students. She said:

> I think the key is the moms. In our culture, the Mexican moms, are really kind of the caregivers of the children and dads aren't as involved as they are, maybe in Anglo homes. Not that they don't want to be, but it's kind of a cultural thing. And so if we can touch these moms and get them moving forward, that's really what we try to do. Help them grow. Help them get more confidence. Help them do some things that maybe they didn't do in the past. Have some resources that they didn't have.

Like the teacher at Putnam, the principal at Stanley contrasted the perceived gender roles in Mexican culture to those within the typical "Anglo" or White American home. She believed that it was the school's role to boost the confidence of Mexican moms, which recalls the assimilationist role of school from earlier eras. She wanted to give Mexican moms skills that would make their children successful:

> Being able to talk to their children, being able to put pressure, sometimes, on their children as far as homework and those kinds of things. It's difficult for some of our moms because they're kind of the comforters and not the pushers.

Again, the principal underlined how Mexican families deviated from mainstream culture. While American norms encourage mothers to be nurturing, the principal believed that Mexican culture went overboard, turning mothers into "comforters" instead of "pushers."

Latino parents were not the only ones teachers perceived as having patriarchal gender roles and attitudes. A White teacher at Dodge was struggling with the patriarchal gender attitudes that she perceived among some of her immigrant families. When asked to describe the parents at her school, she said:

> Mostly wonderful. I go to these parents for parents' meetings and I enjoy meeting people from different cultures. But usually, I hate to say it like this, it's just we have a couple men and they have such a hard time, especially if you are a woman and you say "please." I've learned how to address them.

She began within the ethnic credit frame, saying that she "enjoyed meeting people from different cultures," but moved on to cultural differences that she found more troubling. Her comment that she "hated to say it like this" suggested that the teacher felt uncomfortable about making generalizations about her students' culture, but she did limit the reach of her claim by saying it was only about "a couple of men." However, even a couple of men who hold patriarchal gender attitudes can have an impact, as evidenced by the story she recounted about feeling menaced by a parent:

> Because [one] time we went up to a guy and told him, "Please don't park here," and he got out of the van. A big six foot five guy and just started screaming at us. So I was hiding behind this other guy saying, "Ooh. If he comes over here, please protect us." We had to call the security guard.

Her response suggested that she would not expect the typical American man to react this way toward a woman who asserted herself.

Moreover, while she had not initially associated sexist attitudes with a particular ethnic group, she associated them with Middle Eastern men in the remainder of her comments. She continued:

> But then I met a really wonderful woman from Pakistan. She flagged me down, "You stop, stop." And she said, "Oh I just love it that you're doing this and helping." And she—her idea, because she's lived in the Middle East, was that some people, to tell them what to do is a—takes away from their sense of personal freedom. So they'll fight you unless, you know, you're a policeman. So we're trying to—our new thing is to try to educate people that we're not out to get you. We're just trying to make sure the children are safe. But I think some of the cultures, the man is more dominant so that sometimes is a problem.

She rejected the Pakistani woman's interpretation of why Middle Eastern men did not listen to her. Instead, the teacher attributed their behavior to a patriarchal culture where "the man is more dominant."

Indeed, several teachers believed that South Asian culture was more belligerent and intolerant than (White) American culture. A common theme was that students gained mainstream values from attending American schools. For instance, a White teacher from Dodge said:

> I've got kids from Pakistan and India who are friends in here yet if they were in their own countries, they'd be fighting with each other. So that's a wonderful experience for the kids. It's wonderful for them to be able to grow up in an environment like this.

Another White teacher at Dodge seconded this notion that Pakistani and Indian students learned how to tolerate each other in American schools. While describing the benefits of diversity, she said:

> And it's great with these kids because they all come from countries that have wars.... Pakistani and Indian kids have weapons pointed at one another in their homelands and they're kitchen table discussions. You can tell that these kids they talk to their relatives in their homeland.

She believed the school's diversity counteracted the intolerance that Pakistani and Indian students may have learned when talking to relatives back home and around the kitchen table.

In contrast, teachers associated other Asian cultures with reserve and strictness. These cultural differences did not contradict American values, but they did mark some Asian students as noticeably different from mainstream American society. A Middle Eastern teacher at Dodge seemed to appreciate the strictness of Indian families, but noted that it was different from American families. He explained:

> Western culture says, "Hey I can become a doctors or and we take advantage of that," but if you're from India it's a big privilege to get an education. They can't become surgeons in India so the parents appreciate it. I've had parents tell me "you can hit my kid if you have to," because they think.... They do get hit in India. Education is a big deal and the ones whose parents are screaming and fighting saying their kids have too much homework, the other parents want you to give them more homework.

The teacher constructed Indians as being more appreciative of educational opportunities than Americans, which is another example of teachers crediting immigrant minorities with pro-school attitudes. Yet, he also contended that Indian parents encourage teachers to hit their children to get them to work harder, which might be seen as a more negative deviation from mainstream American behavior.

A White teacher at Bowen subtly contrasted the reserve of one Asian student with the boisterousness of the typical American student. He recounted how a Vietnamese girl in his class struggled to fit in with the other students. He said:

> And she just was a loner, she just ... she'd eat by herself, she'd go to gym, she just was alone all the time. And I thought at first it was a cultural kind of [thing], and I'd call on her and she'd never raise her hand. And I just tried to encourage her, because she's really smart, and she thought that the language would make kids laugh at her.

After asking the class to befriend her, the student became more outgoing, even asking the mayor a question during a fieldtrip. He continued:

> There's a couple of others like that I'm working on. I always say at the beginning, "Down the road, Suzy, I'm gonna have you throwing spitballs across the room." I said "You watch, you watch. You're gonna be running around throwing spitballs and I'm gonna have to say Suzy, I'm gonna call your mother!"

He did not just want Suzy to become more outgoing; he wanted her to be rambunctious like an American student. His image of Suzy's future was more like that of Bart Simpson or Dennis the Menace—iconic, fun-loving American kids. While I doubt that he literally wanted to have to call her mother, he wanted her to do harmless mischief like "throwing spitballs across the room" that was more typical of American than Asian students.

Religion and religiosity was the final factor that separated White and minority immigrants from mainstream culture. The post-1965 waves of immigrants have been more religiously diverse than previous generations (Esser, 2004). Thus, immigrant students differed from mainstream American society because of their faith. Teachers showed the salience of students' faith when they referred to students by their religion. A White teacher at Dodge did this when she said:

> Today someone after we left [a teacher's] room was like, "You know that was sort of boring" and I said "We respect your culture." It was a Moslem boy. I said, "We talk about your holy time and your fasting"'cause I cover all of the . . . I try to cover anything that affects us, and I said, "How would you feel if you heard someone say that when we go through your lesson?"

The student's faith was relevant, since the teacher believed the student was not being as respectful of other cultures as the school had been of his. Still, her comments fit with a pattern where teachers treated students' faith as their most salient identity.

Teachers also believed that immigrant students were more religious than the average American. While students' religiosity gave them "family values," it also set them apart from mainstream American culture. A White teacher at Dodge thought students at his school were more religious than he was at their age:

> Interviewer: How would you say, why do you say that they are a religious group?
> Teacher: Well because I read a lot of their essays but they talk about God a lot, about the Koran and about the Bible. Then they have a fear of God, a higher spirituality, I just feel that way. Once I heard them talking "God

gonna see her." When I was a kid we didn't talk like that, I mean I had a fear of my parents but I would never tell my friends. I can just see it a lot of them are more religious. The Muslim students do go on fasts from sun up to sun down when their fast season . . . some of the kids don't eat until they get home from school. That proves religion there. I have four students who are vegetarians and they only eat special kinds of food for the Muslim. I have had some kids from the Jewish religion to take some days off. I have had kids during Passover who won't eat. So that shows religion.

The teacher noticed his students' religious practices because they were different from his own, such as when he said "they only eat special kinds of food," and because they were more deeply felt, "they have a higher spirituality." He does not cast religiosity as negative, but he does see it as distinctive of his student population.

In contrast, the Asian principal at Dodge was annoyed by the interruptions that religious observances caused, complaining of Pakistani students:

So sometimes they take off like a month for religious holidays or go back home and we have a parent who will take a group of children out for prayer, every Friday for that month. So they have a totally different concept about scheduling.

She would not complain about Christmas break in the same way, because the school observes Christian holidays. Thus, while the principal is not critical of religious difference, she does mark those who are of different faiths and who are highly religious as outsiders.

NOT MIDDLE CLASS

Class has been in the background of much of teachers' talk about the normative student. Teachers talked most explicitly about class when discussing the typical student. They constructed the average student as middle class and associated middle-class status with positive attributes, such as high-achieving students and involved parents. They also constructed middle-class schools as desirable places to teach, particularly suburban schools.

Previous research shows that "middle class" is coded "White" even when racial terms are not used. Often, individuals use the phrases "good students" and "good schools" to combine "middle class" and "White" without having to explicitly use racial and class labels. For instance, a study found that White middle class parents openly defined schools as "good" for being middle class, but admitted when pressed by interviewers that "good" also meant White (Johnson & Shapiro, 2003).

Other research found that scholars associated giftedness with Whiteness and being middle class from its inception, constructing gifted students as "goodness personified" (Margolin, 1993).

Teachers intertwined quality, Whiteness, and being middle class in similar ways in Laketown, typically leaving out the racial category, but implying it. The Black assistant principal at Bowen constructed middle-class students as high achieving while defending the recently hired principal against complaints that the school's achievement had declined. She said, "People that were teachers here long before I came but who were still here when he came were used to the upper-middle-class community with high achieving students." She suggested that middle class meant White in earlier comments, describing the school council that selected the principal as being "a yuppie-ish group" that had "very suburban-like ideas and goals for their kids."

The assistant principal believed that it was misguided for faculty and parents to expect the same level of achievement once the school lost its middle-class population. She figured that the previous principal left the school because she anticipated how the demographic changes would affect the school. She said of the previous principal:

> She had some more traditional views and a lot of these parents, who I was talking about, became council members who had children in Kindergarten. They were just starting and the outlook did not look good for those traditional things staying or the status quo remaining.

"Traditional" is akin to mainstream or normative. Thus, the teacher suggested that the mainstream, middle class, White parents and teachers should have expected a decline in achievement once the school became poorer and had more minority students.

Another individual used Bowen's demographics to justify why the school did not need advanced classes. The White head of the school council at Bowen explained that Korean-American parents were pushing for the school to offer more accelerated classes, saying:

> And given that in the city kids are tempted away by various programs, especially as they get older, and that we wanted to keep good kids. Well, I shouldn't say good kids, but we wanted to keep our top-end kids at Bowen and we wanted to keep them challenged and there was a push from a certain segment of parents in the community, a lot of Korean-Americans in particular, that felt that we should have some sort of accelerated program or gifted program or something like that.

She corrected herself, but the council leader began by labeling high-achieving kids "good kids," which is in keeping with the notion of giftedness as goodness. Interestingly, she cited Korean-American parents as the defenders of high standards, which granted an Asian group the ethnic credit of holding pro-school values.

Yet, she thought it would not be "appropriate" for Bowen to offer many advanced classes, saying: "I mean it is a neighborhood school. We're not going to launch a huge gifted program here despite our feeling like that all our children are above average." She disqualified Bowen from needing advanced classes because it was a "neighborhood school," implying that there were not enough "above average" students to warrant such offerings. When asked if she actually thought many students at Bowen were "above average," the council leader said, "there's a significant number of kids who are very—who are very good and are very bright and need to be challenged." This description of giftedness could cover a wide range of children, yet when pressed, the council leader explained:

> Oh just—well I mean there's a core of really committed people in this neighborhood who are . . . who are educated, middle class, committed to the city, and committed to the school. And I think that our kids probably are above average.

She constructed giftedness as middle class, just as the originators of the gifted category had (Margolin, 1993).

Moreover, her assertion that the children of the middle class are "above average" is unequivocal. Contrast that assertion with her next statement about giftedness:

> So—and then you have this Korean-American group with their, you know . . . personal view. I think they push their kids very hard to achieve in school. And—so they also feel that—and many of their kids are very talented.

The council leader equivocated in her construction of Korean-American students' giftedness. She constructed the giftedness of middle-class kids as something akin to fact, saying they "probably are above average," whereas she constructed the prowess of Korean-American kids as a matter of opinion, saying that Korean-American parents held the "personal view" that "their kids are very talented." Her association between being middle class and being gifted was more definitive.

Teachers also looked to the middle class as the standard for parental behavior, particularly parent involvement. A White teacher at Bowen inadvertently constructed middle-class parents as the standard while explaining why more parents at her school were not involved. She was describing the good, but limited, impact of a grant the school received to pay parents who volunteered at the school.

. . . We weren't going to push it because it wasn't really working because it's very hard to find parents. I mean if they're staying home, it's usually because they have kids and they need to stay home so they can't come in anyways. There's hardly any parents that just stay home because they don't need to work. It's really not like that. It's hardly like that in the suburbs, let alone in a place where you need two incomes because the one income is very low.

She held the suburbs, where presumably both parents earn a decent income, as the standard by which to judge school participation. If middle-class mothers from the suburbs cannot voluntarily stay at home and participate at their children's schools, then Bowen should certainly not expect its low-income parents to participate. By saying the middle-class families cannot even meet the ideal anymore she implied that the ideal was based on them.

A White teacher at Brantley showed that she believed that the middle class was the standard in a similarly indirect way. She was also describing the decline of that middle-class institution, the stay-at-home mom, and the necessity of the two-income family. She said:

I told [another teacher] I said, we should do a book you and I and it should be a book on middle class comes to the projects, because a lot of the kids were going through some of the things that you see out in the suburbs this year. Like their moms because of welfare reform go out to work and so now the kids are latchkey kids, "home alone" comes to the projects.

While welfare reform forced the rise of dual-income families in the "projects," middle-class suburban families had been dealing with the problem of "latchkey kids" for a longer time. The teacher constructed suburban families as typical and her students' families as belatedly confronting problems that were already common in mainstream society.

The school council leader at Dodge whose quote began this chapter drew on both the ethnic credit frame and White privilege to discuss the parents at his school. He assumed that middle-class families would be involved and constructed involvement as typical of them. This assumption is an expression of White privilege that constructs White middle-class behavior as normative and ideal (Perry, 2001). However, after criticizing immigrant families as less involved than the "average middle-class family," he said their reasons for not being involved were legitimate, which granted them ethnic credit for their ethnic difference. Here's the relevant quote:

In fact, I mean the diversity a lot of our ethnic groups don't talk to one another, they don't relate to this being the traditional way—I'm gonna generalize here, in the way your average middle class family does. That it's just natural that you be involved in the PTA or the (school council) type thing, that you volunteer. I mean a lot of the immigrant parents here they're working a lot, they see this as the first stop in their life here in the U.S. A lot of kids are coming here for a couple of years, their parents will get acclimated, they'll get established, their kids will learn English and they'll move on.

As was the case at other schools, he believed that work prevented immigrant families from volunteering in the school council. Still, immigrant parents fall short of the middle-class norm of being involved.

Moreover, he constructed Dodge, an urban school, as an intermediate stop where immigrant families could become "acclimated" to American society before moving on to better things, including, perhaps, better schools. The idea that immigrant families would flee to good suburban schools, as the White middle class had, was taken up by other teachers. The counselor at Dodge also feared that high-achieving immigrant students would leave for the suburbs.

> Interviewer: Now moving on a little bit to parents and community, how would you describe the neighborhood in which the school resides?
>
> Teacher: I've only been here three months, so multi-ethnic. I would say lower-middle class basically. As I mentioned, the high transiency rate. As parents become a little bit more successful, they move on looking for bigger and better things. Not necessarily always to the suburbs, but a lot of times that's where it ends up because I've lost some quality kids to the suburbs.

What is interesting here is that the counselor constructed this flight as inevitable. Perhaps unintentionally, the counselor placed immigrant families within the pattern of White middle-class families, which was to leave the city as soon as possible.

Teachers regarded middle class and suburban schools as the standard of well-functioning, innovative, and safe schools. For example, the Black principal at Martin associated "middle class" with "high-achieving" schools when explaining why Martin and another school were selected for a pilot instructional project. According to the principal, the researchers targeted "University School which is a high achieving, high caliber, primarily middle-class school," and Martin "a regular neighborhood school" to compare the impact of the project.

At Putnam, a White teacher leader associated suburban schools with innovation, saying that while her school had just adopted project-based learning, "The suburbs have been doing it probably for a long time so we're just sort of jumping on the band wagon. . . ." Finally, the White school council chair at Dodge likened the council to children due to their "passive aggressive" relationship with the principal. He suggested that this dysfunction was a "Laketown thing," saying that ". . .

I work with suburban schools but I don't know the dynamics that well. [They] are just simply really passive aggressive about stuff." He was frustrated that the council did not deal more directly with conflict. His parting remarks were, "People aren't very good at that in Laketown. For being adults they're not good at it."

Nevertheless, several teachers preferred urban schools to suburban, middle-class schools. Many teachers, like the council leader from Bowen, had grown up in the city and wanted to return. This exchange with a White teacher at Dodge was typical of teachers who felt drawn to urban schools because of their location:

> Interviewer: Was there anything about Dodge that made you choose this school?
>
> Teacher: I had a friend who was here and told me there were three vacancies about to come up so I hustled and got my stuff and was ready to come back. I had only taught in suburban and small towns, I taught in upstate New York, and being a city girl, a graduate of city high schools and elementary school, it was nice to be back in the city.

An Asian-American teacher at Bowen acknowledged this trend of White flight back to the city. She said good schools like hers were becoming overcrowded by middle-class families returning to cities like Laketown:

> I think it is the trend and the baby boomers are filling up the classrooms and there is a move to come back and live in the city because they have made the city so nice now. The people are no longer moving to the suburbs for their good schools they are demanding that it be here in the city and in Laketown, they just built that nice prep school on the north side and all these magnet schools are here to accommodate the more affluent needs, when they have traditionally gone to the suburbs.

Teachers were also part of this trend; they were returning to the city looking for good schools in which to teach.

Indeed, a few teachers believed that their particular urban school rivaled the quality of suburban schools. A White teacher at Dodge thought that her colleagues were as good as those at any school. She said the teachers were "great" when the interviewer asked what she thought of them and that she "marveled at how much talent there is." In fact, she confided:

> And I'll tell you frankly I would have no problems sending my kids to this school. I really wouldn't. I'm out in the suburbs where supposedly everything's so wonderful. But I see better teaching here than I see in my own kids' school.

That is a strong endorsement of urban schools, but it only covered her school, not urban schools as a whole.

Similarly, a White teacher at Stanley was also critical of the notion that suburban schools in general were better than her particular urban school. When asked about her career, she said:

> . . . I would not think of going anywhere else at this point. I'm very happy here. And I'm glad that I'm here. I think this is a, I think this is an excellent school. And I think it's a good model school for not only city schools, but suburban as well because I, where I live I can compare what goes on and I say it constantly, "that would never happen in my school." Because I know how things work over here.

As someone who lived in the suburbs, the teacher knew her school was better than suburban schools and could be a model for them. Still, other comments by the teacher suggested that she did not think urban students were typically good. She recalled being duped into thinking that the first school in which she taught would be good because it was located in the suburbs, only to find out it was populated by students bussed in from the city. She said:

> My first year teaching I got a job at a school on the northwest side of Laketown and I thought I was, I thought I hit the jackpot because the school was in the middle of this Laketown suburb, with all the ranch houses and it had this sprawling lawn in the front and I thought "Wow, this looks like a great school in a great neighborhood, it's going to be great kids." Well, it turned out to be a dumping ground school. It was a school where the kids were bussed in from overcrowded schools in the city.

The teacher expected the suburban school, with trappings of middle-class status like "ranch houses" and a "sprawling lawn," would have "great kids." Instead, she found unmotivated city kids "who did not want to be there." Her dream suburban school was actually a "nightmare" because it was full of urban students.

Her comments showed the limits of teachers' praise of urban schools. Teachers at multiracial and Latino schools elevated the status of their own schools, but did not question the low status of urban schools and students in general. Moreover, even teachers who valued their own urban schools also bought into the idea that suburban schools were better. Thus, while *some* teachers valued the unique attractions of urban schools, including their diversity and their location, *most* teachers valued the benefits they expected from middle-class, suburban schools: high-achieving students, involved parents, and well-functioning, instructionally sound schools.

Teachers' talk about middle-class students and schools made clear the difference between ethnic credits and racial privilege. While teachers varied in whether they constructed immigrant status as positive, they almost always constructed middle-class (White) students in positive ways. This did not mean that teachers always preferred middle-class students, since a vocal group of teachers across schools actually preferred urban schools and diverse students. Yet, even these teachers acknowledged that middle-class schools were seen as the ideal and consciously justified their preference for poorer, more minority-populated schools. Thus, all teachers, no matter what type of schools they preferred, constructed middle-class students as desirable and normative. Ethnic credits were contingent on teachers recognizing ethnic difference as valuable, but teachers almost always constructed (White) middle-class status as valuable.

CHAPTER 6

Fulfilling the Promise of Diversity

"In many cases, minority children, ours are predominantly Hispanic, but I think also African Americans and other minority groups, they're put in a box, they're labeled . . . with a lot of negative things. People don't think they can be successful simply because of the color of their skin or the fact that their first language is not English or whatever it is. I think our society has not put high expectations on minority children so I really want our children to have the option to do whatever they want."

—White principal at Stanley, a Latino school

What do teachers think about the racial and ethnic diversity of their schools? According to the teachers in this book, they love it, as long as it is diversity of the right type. While the balance of the book is about the underside of this view, we should note how unexpected it was that teachers valued diversity in the first place. After all, research shows that teachers prefer White middle-class schools to Black or Latino ones (Groulx, 2001) and that they have negative perceptions of Black and Latino students (though not of Asian-American students) (Rosenbloom & Way, 2004). Thus, the practice of valuing difference set these teachers apart from teachers in other research.

Moreover, while I am critical of the practice, assimilating diversity is an improvement over the Jim Crow racism that treated minorities as inferior and saw nothing valuable about students of color. It also departs from the assimilation of the early 20th century, which insisted that students of color erase their difference to be incorporated into American society, and from the pluralism of the 1950s and 1960s that said that minority culture only benefitted minorities, not the dominant group (Tyack, 2003). The practice of assimilating diversity could only emerge after America officially renounced racism and embraced multiculturalism as a sign of its commitment to tolerance. In that sense, assimilating diversity is an index of how far we have come from the bad old days of overt racism.

In fact, teachers developed habits of thinking about difference that could be expanded to benefit all minorities. For instance, teachers valued at least some forms of difference, a practice that could be extended to see value in all minority groups. They also believed that they should learn about their students' backgrounds. While teachers did not claim the influence of culturally relevant pedagogy, they nevertheless stumbled onto one of its central tenets for how best to teach students of color (Ladson-Billings, 1997). Namely, teachers recognized that they were not the only experts, but instead treated students as though they had valued knowledge, if only about their own culture.

Teachers also showed an appreciation for teaching at certain types of urban minority schools. They sought out schools with large populations of students of color. This taste for difference could help retain teachers at other minority schools, which are traditionally hard to staff and have high turnover (Frankenberg, 2006). Finally, teachers developed the habit of staying committed to teaching disadvantaged students and to recognizing their strengths in the face of adversity. These habits could be extended to create a more supportive educational environment for all minority students.

Yet, the practices that constituted assimilating diversity, using an ethnic paradigm of race, focusing on how diversity benefits the dominant group, and reproducing White normativity, had significant shortcomings. The rest of this book shows why diversity has been such a seductive and omnivorous paradigm for making sense of minority status, gobbling up older paradigms such as social justice and anti-racism and replacing aspirations of equality with aspirations of tolerance and mutual benefit. This chapter reviews some of the key shortcomings of the practice of assimilating diversity. Ultimately, this book finds that diversity, as filtered through color blind multiculturalism, held hidden injuries for both African Americans and immigrant minorities.

The quote that begins this chapter points in a different direction. It suggests what could happen if schools were to fulfill the promise of diversity to promote not just tolerance, but social justice. The principal at Stanley did not shy away from the language of inequality; she recognized that society has negative stereotypes of racial minorities "because of the color of their skin." Moreover, she politicized immigrant status by saying that society had negative stereotypes of immigrant minorities because "their first language isn't English." In these ways, she broke with color blind multiculturalism by focusing on racial, not just ethnic, difference and by acknowledging power dynamics that structure how Americans react to minority status. Her perceptions of minority students were driven by social justice and anti-racist ideologies and were geared toward recognizing obstacles that native-born and immigrant minorities shared in common, rather than elevating one group above another.

The remainder of this chapter is written in the spirit of her quote. It imagines how diversity could be done differently, such that it values all minority groups and recognizes their struggles and their strengths. I describe an alternate approach to diversity that is aimed toward social justice. This approach is informed by Critical Race Theory (Dixson & Rousseau, 2005). Rather than playing racial and ethnic groups against each other, this approach advocates recognizing cultures of achievement among different minority groups (Neckerman, Carter, & Lee, 1999).

It extends the asset-focused frame that teachers used with immigrant minorities to include Blacks and encourages teachers to recognize resilience across minority groups (Clegg, 2011). Moreover, the approach reintroduces politics into the perception of difference by acknowledging that structures of inequality have negative effects on minority groups.

ORTHODOX INEQUALITY: HOW ASSIMILATING DIVERSITY REINFORCES SOCIAL HIERARCHIES

I was surprised to find that the schools that I studied could be characterized by a single racial orthodoxy, assimilating diversity. This common orthodoxy meant that teachers at a multiracial school like Dodge had a similar view of difference as teachers at a Latino school like Stanley. At both schools, teachers valued the ethnic difference they associated with immigrant minorities like Asians and Latinos and rewarded students with symbolic benefits as a result. At the same time, assimilating diversity rendered Black students valueless at multiracial schools and concentrated the stigma at Black schools.

DOING DIVERSITY DIFFERENTLY

Teachers would have to change at least two aspects of how they thought about difference in order to recognize the value of all minority groups. They would need to change their ideology from color blind multiculturalism to one that recognized power and inequality. In addition, they would have to adapt a discourse that recognized strengths across minority groups. These represent fundamental deviations from how the teachers in this book thought about difference, yet are in keeping with their evident desire to behave in a just and tolerant way toward minorities.

Bringing Power Back In

Color blind multiculturalism was the ideology that drove assimilating diversity; it was the glue that held its disparate practices together. As practices, celebrating difference, as multiculturalism calls for us to do, and focusing on how diversity benefits the dominant group need not preserve the status quo. However, color blindness limited the progressive potential of multiculturalism by ignoring how race was a source of inequality, not just useful difference. Color blindness depoliticized difference and reduced ethnic identity to a matter of enriching cultural values and beliefs. Thus, it is the combination of color blindness and multiculturalism that reduced the progressive potential of assimilating diversity.

Teachers would have to change their ideology to one that recognized the role of power in social identities. Teachers would not need to abandon their appreciation of ethnic differences, but they would be better able to recognize the implications of the distinctions they made between minority groups. However, they would have to break with the ethnic paradigm of race, which treats race and ethnicity as voluntary identities that have no social consequences (Gallagher, 2003). Instead, they would have to acknowledge how race and ethnicity shape the life chances of their students in ways that both enable and constrain them.

The White principal at Stanley clearly recognized that race and ethnicity were structures of power. She was able to see strengths in Latino students, but she was also attuned to racialized obstacles they faced. Her positive view of Latinos was especially noteworthy because it was not grounded in shared racial heritage, as were the positive perceptions of Black teachers at Black schools. While she was just one example, she shows that White faculty could adopt an anti-racist perspective. Anti-racist teaching practices are not new, but this book shows that multiculturalism and anti-racism are not interchangeable. It suggests that teachers should not substitute multiculturalism for anti-racism or any other ideology that does not have social justice at its core (Nieto, 1996; Sleeter, 1993).

A final quote shows that faculty has different concerns when they adopt a social justice perspective. The principal at Stanley believed that society viewed her students' troubles learning English through a deficit-oriented, racialized lens. As a result, she made writing a cornerstone of Stanley's pedagogy and had all her students write essays throughout the year that she read and edited personally. She described the need for this labor-intensive process in terms that acknowledged school as an arena for racial struggle, saying:

> Well, it's part of my whole drive about perceptions that people have of minority children. And, you know, being able to speak and being able to write are two very important components of people perceiving you as being an educated person. And I think sometimes in the hustle and bustle of teaching on a day-to-day basis, people forget that there are some real critical components to the perception of excellence for kids.

Instead of being color blind, the principal was race-conscious. She knew that race mattered in how students were perceived. She designed the curriculum at Stanley to address the symbolism of their education, not just their practical needs. Yet, by taking race into account, the principal mandated that her students exceed the amount of writing that most schools required. A truly tolerant society can acknowledge student differences without reading those differences as lack. We can imagine another model of diversity, one that does not pit races against each other, but rather recognizes differences without ranking them.

Adopting a Discourse of Resilience

The teacher's most marked characteristic was that they perceived strength in their minority students' difference. Yet, they only recognized strengths within one group, immigrant minorities. Teachers were on the right track, though. They were aware of some of the difficulties that students faced, such as lack of parental involvement or living in dangerous neighborhoods. Yet, instead of dwelling on what students did not have, they saw resilience in the way students overcame these obstacles.

There is no reason that teachers could not extend this line of thinking to native-born minority groups. However, teachers would have to develop a new discourse that could recognize strengths in a range of groups. Scholars have already begun to identify behaviors that differ between immigrant and native-born minorities, but still lead to academic achievement (Neckerman et al., 1999). Teachers would benefit if they knew more about the different cultures of achievement among minority groups.

Moreover, teachers would need a new language for understanding class differences to recognize resilience across groups. We saw that the particular meaning that Black poverty held dampened teacher perceptions of Black students. Even Black teachers who otherwise had social justice orientations saw Black students' families through a culture of poverty lens. Where teachers saw resilience in poor Latino students, they only saw deviance in poor Black students. This could be changed if we developed a language that de-pathologized poverty, particularly of Blacks. Scholars in England have already begun theorizing how teachers could recognize the strengths within working-class and poor British students (Clegg, 2011). Scholars in the United States could do similar work.

These changes to how teachers think about diversity are modest, but they could make a big difference in what difference means. At base, the changes envision a world where teachers would not mark any racial or ethnic identity as the wrong kind of difference. To get to that place, teachers would have to abandon color blindness as a comforting, but pernicious, myth. They would have to recognize the harm that is caused when they compare minority groups to each other without a grasp of how race and ethnicity structure society.

As a remedy for intolerance, assimilating diversity is a cure that is worse than the illness. It cements hierarchies between racial minorities and reinforces White normativity while seeming to do the opposite. Because assimilating diversity appears progressive, it is harder to combat and easier to entrench. As an orthodox discourse, it forecloses other ways of thinking about difference and minority status that may benefit students of color more. Yet, teachers' ability to value some minority students may be a first step toward developing another perspective that recognizes the unique strengths and struggles of all groups.

Methodology

This book is based on an analysis of one year of data from the Distributed Leadership Study (DLS), a 4-year qualitative study of leadership at 11 elementary schools across a large Midwestern city. I was the primary ethnographer at one of the schools and had access to the data on all of the other schools. I analyzed interviews with 100 teachers and leaders from all 11 schools. The teachers were 2nd and 5th grade math, reading, and science instructors.

Schools varied by student racial composition: seven were Black, two were Latino, and two were multiracial. Multiracial schools were defined as schools where no racial/ethnic group made up more than half of the student population, while minority schools were defined as schools with 80 to 100% of the minority group. Schools also varied by class composition: There were three middle-class schools and eight poor schools, based on the percentage of students receiving free lunch. The sample was representative of the composition of schools in the city (see Table 1.1).

Semi-structured interviews were conducted with leaders and teachers before and after teaching lessons. All interviews were transcribed and entered into QSR NUD*IST, a qualitative data management program. I read all transcripts for references to students, then I identified interviews with references to students' race or ethnicity. The analysis of these comments is the basis of the research. Importantly, these were unprompted comments about race and ethnicity, since the DLS was not designed to study race and ethnicity. Most of these comments occurred when teachers were asked about how a lesson went and about the strengths and weaknesses of the students, parents, and community. I coded teachers as having positive or negative perceptions depending on whether they focused on students' strengths or weaknesses.

I used racial labels (e.g., Black or Asian) and ethnic labels (e.g., Russian or Mexican) and code words to categorize teachers' discourse as ethnicizing or racializing. (Code words are common signifiers that signal racial or ethnic thinking without explicitly naming a minority group [Frankenberg, 1993]). Coding for labels and code words yielded a sample of 130 interviews with references to race and ethnicity (including Whites and others). Table 1.2 shows the teacher demographics. As in most American cities, there were more White teachers in the sample than teachers of any other race, followed by Black and then Latino teachers (Frankenberg, 2006). There were only a handful of Asian teachers.

Narratives are standard stories that individuals tell themselves to make sense of social phenomena (Bonilla-Silva, Lewis, & Embrick, 2004). Racial and ethnic narratives have plotlines that explain inequality between Whites and people of color. Ethnic narratives were ones that focused on the effects of immigrant status (such as being bilingual) and on cultural inheritances from national origins (such as community-mindedness). Racial narratives were ones that focused on the impact of race and other structural barriers and treated difference as immutable. Teachers tended to use ethnic narratives to talk about Asians and Latinos and racial narratives when talking about Blacks.

References

Alexander, K., Entwisle, D., & Thompson, M. S. (1987). School performance, status relations, and the structure of sentiment: Bringing the teacher back in. *American Sociological Review, 52*(5), 665–682.

Archer, L., & Francis, B. (2005). "They never go off the rails like other ethnic groups": Teachers' constructions of British Chinese pupils' gender identities and approaches to learning. *British Journal of Sociology of Education, 26*(2), 165–182.

Bankston, C. L. I. (2004). Social capital, cultural values, immigration, and academic achievement: The host country context and contradictory consequences. *Sociology of Education, 77*(2), 176–79.

Bell, J. M., & Hartmann, D. (2007). Diversity in everyday discourse: The cultural ambiguities and consequences of "happy talk." *American Sociological Review, 72*(6), 895–914.

Berrey, E. C. (2011). Why diversity became orthodox in higher education, and how it changed the meaning of race on campus. *Critical Sociology, 37*(5), 573–596.

Bonilla-Silva, E. (2003). *Racism without racists: Color-blind racism and the persistence of racial inequality in the United States.* Lanham, MD: Rowan & Littlefield.

Bonilla-Silva, E. (2004). From bi-racial to tri-racial: Towards a new system of racial stratification in the USA. *Ethnic and Racial Studies, 27*(6), 931–950. doi:10.1080/0141987042000268530

Bonilla-Silva, E., Lewis, A., & Embrick, D. G. (2004). "I did not get that job because of a Black man . . . ": The story lines and testimonies of color-blind racism. *Sociological Forum, 19*(4), 555–581.

Bourdieu, P. (1984). *Distinction: A social critique of the judgment of taste.* Cambridge, MA: Harvard University Press.

Bullivant, B. M. (1988). The ethnic success ethic: Ubiquitous phenomenon in English-speaking societies? *Ethnic and Racial Studies, 11*(1), 63–84.

Casteel, C. A. (1998). Teacher-student interactions and race in integrated classrooms. *Journal of Educational Research, 92* (2), 115–120.

Chicago Public Schools. (2000). *Racial Ethnic Survey, School Year 2000–2001.*

Clegg, S. (2011). Cultural capital and agency: Connecting critique and curriculum in higher education. *British Journal of Sociology of Education, 32*(1), 93–108. doi:10.108 0/01425692.2011.527723

Cooper, E., & Allen, M. (1998). A meta-analytic examination of the impact of student race on classroom interaction. *Communication Research Reports, 15*(2), 151–161.

Devine, D. (2005). Welcome to the Celtic tiger? Teacher responses to immigration and increasing diversity in Irish schools. *International Studies in Sociology of Education*, *15*(1), 49–70.

Diamond, J., & Spillane, J. (2004). Teachers' expectations and sense of responsibility for student learning: The implications of school, race, class, and organizational habits. *Anthropology and Education Quarterly*, *35*(1), 75–98.

Dixson, A., & Rousseau, C. (2005). And we are still not saved: Critical race theory in education ten years later. *Race, Ethnicity and Education*, *8*(1), 7–27.

DuBois, W. E. B. (2007). *The Souls of Black Folk*. New York: Cosimo Classics.

Ehrenberg, R., & Brewer, D. J. (1995). Do teachers' race, gender and ethnicity matter? Evidence from the national educational longitudinal study of 1988. *Industrial and Labor Relations Review*, *48*(3), 547–561.

Embrick, D. (2011). The diversity ideology in the business world : A new oppression for a new age. *Critical Sociology*. doi:10.1177/0896920510380076

Esser, H. (2004). Does the "new" immigration require a "new" theory of intergenerational integration? *International Migration Review*, *38*(3), 1126–1159.

Farkas, G., Sheehan, D., Grobe, R. P., & Shuan, Y. (1990). Cultural resources and school success: Gender, ethnicity, and poverty groups within an urban school district. *American Sociological Review*, *55* (1), 148–155.

Farley, J. E. (2005). *Majority-minority relations* (5th ed.). Upper Saddle River, NJ: Prentice Hall.

Fass, P. S. (1989). *Outside in: Minorities and the transformation of American education*. New York: Oxford University Press.

Ferguson, R. F. (1998). Teachers' perceptions and expectations and the Black-White test score gap. In C. J. Phillips & Meredith (Eds.), *The Black-White test score gap*. Washington, DC: Brookings Institution Press.

Fordham, S., & Ogbu, J. (1986). Black Students' School Success: Coping with the "Burden of Acting White." *Urban Review*, *18*, 176–206.

Foster, M. (1998). *Black teachers on teaching*. New Press Education Series. New York: New Press.

Frankenberg, E. (2006). *The segregation of American teachers*. Cambridge, MA: The Civil Rights Project at Harvard University.

Frankenberg, R. (1993). *White women, race matters: The social construction of Whiteness*. Minneapolis: University of Minnesota.

Freeman, D. J., Brookhart, S. M., & Loadman, W. E. (1999). Realities of teaching in racially/ethnically diverse schools: Feedback from entry-level teachers. *Urban Education*, *34*(1), 89–114.

Gallagher, C. (2003). Playing the ethnic card: Using ethnic identity to negate contemporary racism. In A. Doane & E. Bonilla-Silva (Eds.), *White out: The continuing significance of racism* (pp. 145–158). New York: Routledge.

Garner, R. (2007). Segregation in Chicago. *The Tocqueville Review/ La Revue Tocqueville*, *28*(1), 41–73.

Gay, G. (2000). *Culturally Responsive Teaching : Theory, Research, and Practice*. New York: Teachers College Press.

Goffman, E. (1986). *Stigma: Notes on the Management of Spoiled Identity* (1st ed.). New York: Touchstone.

Groulx, J. G. (2001). Changing preservice teacher perceptions of minority schools. *Urban Education, 36*(1), 60–92.

Guglielmo, T. A. (2003). *White on arrival: Italians, race, color, and power in Chicago, 1890–1945*. New York: Oxford University Press.

Hsu, R. Y. (1996). "Will the model minority please identify itself?" American ethnic identity and its discontents. *Diaspora: A Journal of Transnational Studies, 5*(1), 37–64.

Jacobson, M. F. (1999). *Whiteness of a different color: European immigrants and the alchemy of race*. Cambridge, MA: Harvard University Press.

Jacobson, M. F. (2008). *Roots too: White ethnic revival in post-civil rights America*. Cambridge, MA: Harvard University Press.

Johnson, H. B., & Shapiro, T. M. (2003). Good neighborhoods, good schools: Race and the "good choices" of White families. In E. Bonilla-Silva & W. Doane (Eds.), *White out: The continuing significance of racism* (pp. 173–187). New York: Routledge.

Jung, M.-K. (2009). The racial unconscious of assimilation theory. *Du Bois Review: Social Science Research on Race, 6*(2), 375–395. doi:10.1017/S1742058X09990245

Kim, C. J. (1999). The racial triangulation of Asian Americans. *Politics & Society, 27*(1), 105 –138.

Ladson-Billings, G. (1996). "Your blues ain't like mine": Keeping issues of race and racism on the multicultural agenda. *Theory into Practice, 35*(4), 248–255.

Ladson-Billings, G. (1997). *The dreamkeepers: Successful teachers of African American children*. San Francisco: Jossey-Bass.

Margolin, L. (1993). Goodness personified: The emergence of gifted children. *Social Problems, 40*(4), 510–532.

McBride, D. (2005). *Why I hate Abercrombie & Fitch: Essays on race and sexuality*. New York: NYU Press.

McCarthy, C. (1993). Beyond the poverty of theory in race relations: Nonsynchronicity and social difference in education. In L. Weis & M. Fine (Eds.), *Beyond silenced voices: Class, race and gender in U.S. schools*. Albany, NY: State University of New York Press.

Mueller, C. W., & Price, J. L. (1999). The effects of group racial composition on job satisfaction, organizational commitment, and career commitment: The case of teachers. *Work and Occupations, 26*(2), 187–219.

Myers, K. A., & Williamson, P. (2001). Race talk: The perpetuation of racism through private discourse. *Race and Society, 4*(1), 3–26.

Neckerman, K., Carter, P. L., & Lee, J. (1999). Segmented assimilation and minority cultures of mobility. *Ethnic and Racial Studies, 22*(6), 945–965.

The New London Group. (1996). A pedagogy of multiliteracies: Designing social futures. *Harvard Educational Review, 66*(1), 60–92.

Nieto, S. (1996). *Affirming diversity: The sociopolitical context of multicultural education* (2nd ed.). White Plains, NY: Longman Publishers.

O'Connor, C. (2001). Making sense of the complexity of social identity in relation to achievement: A sociological challenge in the new millennium. *Sociology of Education, Extra Issue,* 159–168.

Ogbu, J. (1995). Cultural problems in minority education: Their interpretations and consequences. Part one: Theoretical background. *The Urban Review, 27,* 189–205.

Olneck, M. R. (1990). The recurring dream: Symbolism and ideology in intercultural and multicultural education. *American Journal of Education, 98*(2), 147–174.

Omi, M., & Winant, H. (1994). *Racial formation in the United States: From the 1960s to the 1990s* (2nd ed.). New York: Routledge.

Perry, P. (2001). White means never having to say you're ethnic. *Journal of Contemporary Ethnography, 30*(1), 56–91. doi:10.1177/089124101030001002

Pierre, J. (2004). Black immigrants in the United States and the "cultural narratives" of ethnicity. *Identities, 11*(2), 141–170.

Pollock, M. (2001). How the question we ask about race in education is the very question we most suppress. *Educational Researcher, 30* (9), 2–12.

Pollock, M. (2004). Race wrestling: Struggling strategically with race in educational practice and research. *American Journal of Education, 111*(1), 25–67.

Reay, D., Hollingworth, S., Williams, K., Crozier, G., Jamieson, F., James, D., & Beedell, P. (2007). "A darker shade of pale?" Whiteness, the middle classes and multi-ethnic inner city schooling. *Sociology, 41*(6), 1041–1060. doi:10.1177/0038038507082314

Rist, R. (1970). Student social class and teacher expectations: The self-fulfilling prophecy in ghetto education. *Harvard Educational Review, 40*(3), 411–451.

Rosenbloom, S. R., & Way, N. (2004). Experiences of discrimination among African American, Asian American and Latino adolescents in an urban high school. *Youth and Society, 35*(4), 420–451.

Sleeter, C. E. (1993). How White teachers construct race. In C. McCarthy & W. Crichlow (Eds.), *Race, Identity, and Representation in Education* (pp. 157–171). New York: Routledge.

Sleeter, C. E. (2000). Epistemological diversity in research on preservice teacher preparation for historically underserved children. *Review of Research in Education, 25*(1), 209.

Tyack, D. (2003). *Seeking common ground: Public schools in a diverse society.* Cambridge, MA: Harvard University Press.

Walters, P. B. (1999). Education and advancement: Exploring the hopes and dreams of Blacks and poor Whites at the turn of the century. In M. Lamont (Ed.), *The Cultural Territories of Race: Black and White Boundaries* (pp. 268–288). Chicago: The University of Chicago Press.

Warikoo, N. (2004). Race and the teacher-student relationship: Interpersonal connections between West Indian students and their teachers in a New York City high school. *Race Ethnicity and Education, 7*(2), 135–147.

Index

Achievement
  at-risk kids and, 35–37
  decent immigrant narrative and, 30
  dividing up differences and, 9, 12,
    13–14, 15–16, 17
  ethnic credits and racial penalties and,
    27–30, 35–37, 41
  ethnicizing minority status and, 17
  good and bad diversity and, 52
  history of race and ethnicity and, 12,
    13–14
  immigrant status as burden narrative
    and, 27–30
  language barriers and, 27–30
  in multiracial schools, 52, 64
  promise of diversity and, 108–109, 111
  social cost of minority status and, 41
  stigma against Black schools and, 63,
    64, 72
  values and, 29, 30
  White norm and, 87, 99, 100–101, 103
"Acting White," 65
Affirmative Action, 18
After-school programs, 38
Alexander, K., 16, 23, 46
Allen, M., 16
American-ness, White norm and, 5, 90–93
Americanization, as goal of education, 91
Archer, L., 14
Asians
  consequences of disparities in teacher
    perceptions of minorities and, 15
  dividing up differences and, 2, 9, 10, 12,
    15, 17, 18, 19, 20, 107, 109

as DLS teachers, 113
ethnic credits and racial penalities and,
  2, 23, 24, 25, 30, 31, 41
good and bad diversity and, 44–45, 49,
  50, 51, 52, 54–55
history of race and ethnicity and, 12
Laketown demographics and, 19, 20
as "model minority," 17
multiculturalism and, 84
multiracial schools and, 44–45, 49, 50,
  51, 52, 54–55
narratives about, 24, 25, 30–31, 114
as perpetual immigrants, 3
White norm and, 18, 88, 89, 96, 97, 98,
  99, 101, 104
See also specific topic
Assimilating diversity
  characteristics of, 4
  colorblind multiculturalism as driver of,
    109–110
  components of, 17–18
  definition of, 8
  democracy and, 21
  dividing up differences and, 4, 8–9,
    17–18
  ethnic credits and racial penalties and,
    25
  good and bad diversity and, 44
  orthodox inequality and, 109–111
  practices for, 8–9
  promise of diversity and, 5, 107–108,
    109–111
  shortcomings of, 108–111
  White norm and, 4, 88

Assimilation
    dividing up differences and, 11–12,
        13–14
    good and bad diversity and, 61
    history of race and ethnicity and, 11–12,
        13–14
    promise of diversity and, 107
    as solution to problem of diversity, 1
    White norm and, 88, 90–93, 95
At-risk kids narrative, 25, 27, 35–37

Bankston, C.L.I., 9, 15
Basic skills, at Black schools, 78–80, 82
Beedel, P., 5, 18, 44
Bell, J. M., 5, 10, 47
Berrey, E. C., 8, 10, 17, 18
Bilingualism
    discontents of diversity and, 59–60
    good and bad diversity and, 58, 59–60,
        61
    immigrant status as burden narrative
        and, 27–29
    multiracial schools and, 58, 59–60, 61
    White norm and, 90
"Black boys in crisis" narrative, 34–35
Black history, 81
Black History Month, 81
Black schools
    basic skills at, 78–80, 82
    Black culture and, 81, 84
    Blackness at, 2–3, 68–70, 85
    celebrations of students' heritages at, 81,
        84
    challenges facing teachers at, 78–84
    characteristics/demographics of, 5, 20
    concentrated stigma at, 3, 68–71, 85, 109
    discipline in, 78, 79, 82–84
    and diversity as leaving Black schools
        behind, 84–85
    as exceptionally good, 5, 72–74
    faculty at, 1, 65, 68–69, 85
    first experiences teaching in, 67–68

    good and bad diversity and, 85
    "kids are just kids" strategy and, 72,
        75–78
    outsider status of White teachers at,
        70–71
    promise of diversity and, 109, 110
    race conscious environment in, 80–82
    reluctance of teachers to teach in, 64
    as reminders of America's past, 63
    society's negative perceptions of, 65–66
    stereotypes of, 64
    stigma against, 1, 2–3, 5, 9, 63–85
    symbolic burden of teaching at, 65–66,
        72–78
    teacher-student relationships at, 71
    unique needs of, 78–84
    as the "worst of the worst," 67
    See also specific school
Black teachers
    burden of teaching black and, 72–78
    discipline and, 82–84
    as discontents of diversity, 58–59
    ethnic credits and racial penalties and,
        27, 29, 30–31, 32, 33, 34, 35, 36,
        37, 38, 39, 41, 42
    good and bad diversity and, 43, 44, 47,
        48, 50, 54, 58–59, 60
    multiracial schools and, 43, 44, 47, 48,
        50, 54, 58–59, 60
    narratives of, 27, 29, 30–31, 32, 33, 34,
        35, 36, 37, 38, 39, 41, 42
    promise of diversity and, 110, 111
    in sample of DLS, 113
    stigma against Black schools and, 1, 3,
        70–71, 72–78, 84
    White norm and, 89, 94
    White teachers as outsiders and, 70–71
    See also specific school
Blacks
    as demonized minority group, 63
    as different, not foreign, 45
    historical treatment of, 10–14

See also Black schools; Black teachers;
    specific topic
Bonilla-Silva, E., 8, 9, 93, 94, 114
Bourdieu, P., 40
Bowen Elementary School (multiracial
    school)
    attraction of diversity for teachers at,
        46–47
    demographics of, 20, 21, 45–46, 52
    and first experiences teaching at Black
        schools, 68, 71
    good and bad diversity and, 44–47,
        48–53, 54, 56–57, 58, 59, 60
    Laketown demographics and, 44–45
    reputation of, 45
    teachers at, 21
    teaching for student deficits and, 79, 80
    White norm and, 97, 100–102, 104
Brantley Elementary School (Black school),
    20, 21, 67–68, 69, 70, 71, 75–77,
    79–80, 102
Brewer, D. J., 14
Brookhart, S. M., 16, 67
Bullivant, B. M., 14

Caring, students as, 31
Carter, P. L., 108, 111
Casteel, C. A., 16, 46
Chicago Public Schools, 67
Chorus
    stigma against Black schools and, 65
    teachers' use of, 49, 50–51
Clegg, S., 109, 111
Climate, school, 15–16, 84
Clumping, stigma against Black schools
    and, 72
Colorblind multiculturalism
    dividing up differences and, 85
    as driver of assimilating diversity,
        109–110
    good and bad diversity and, 43, 53, 58
    multiracial schools and, 43, 53, 58, 85

promise of diversity and, 108, 109–10
    stigma against Black schools and, 63,
        84, 85
    White norm and, 91
Colorblindness
    dividing up differences and, 7, 8, 17, 18
    good and bad diversity and, 55, 57, 58, 61
    in multiracial schools, 55, 57, 58, 61
    need for abandonment of, 111
    productive diversity and, 18
    promise of diversity and, 111
    proper racial talk and, 7
    shortcomings of, 3–4
    stigma against Black schools and, 76,
        77, 85
    teachers response to diversity and, 1
    theorizing racial orthodoxy in Laketown
        and, 17
    White norm and, 93
    See also Colorblind multiculturalism
Community
    culture of poverty narratives and, 32
    decent immigrant narrative and, 32
    ethnic credits and racial penalties and, 23,
        28, 31, 32, 41
    good and bad diversity and, 55, 56–57
    immigrant status as burden and, 28
    impact on leadership practices of, 31
    multiracial schools and, 55, 56–57, 64
    social cost of minority status and, 41
    stigma against Black schools and, 64, 73,
        76–77, 85
Conflict., *See also* Racial harmony
Cooper, E., 16
Cosmopolitanism, 44, 48–53
Critical Race Theory, 108–109
Crozier, G., 5, 18, 44
Culturally relevant pedagogy, 78, 80–81,
    82, 107
Culture
    benefits of diversity and, 1
    decent immigrants narrative and, 30

Culture (*continued*)
    diversity as appreciation of unfamiliar, 2
    dividing up differences and, 9, 17
    ethnic credits and racial penalties and,
        23, 30
    ethnicizing minority status and, 17
    promise of diversity and, 107–109
    White norm and, 90–99
    See also Culture of poverty narrative;
        Multiculturalism
Culture of poverty narrative
    ethnic, 23, 25–27, 33
    ethnic credits and racial penalties and,
        13, 25–27, 32–35, 42
    racial, 23, 25, 26, 32–35
    social cost of minority status and, 42
    with-in school solutions to, 27
Curiosity, perils of colorblind thinking
    and, 3
Curriculum
    dividing up differences and, 12
    good and bad diversity and, 53–54, 60
    history of race and ethnicity and, 12
    multiracial schools and, 53–54, 60
    promise of diversity and, 110
    stigma against Black schools and, 81

Danger
    culture of poverty narratives and, 25,
        26–27, 32
    promise of diversity and, 111
    See also Violence
Decent immigrant narrative, 23, 26, 30–32
Deficits, student, stigma against Black
    schools and, 78–80
Democracy
    assimilating diversity and, 21
    dividing up differences and, 8, 11, 12,
        13, 21
    ethnic credits and racial penalties and, 24
    history of race and ethnicity and, 13
    stigma against Black schools and, 85
Devine, D., 14

Diamond, J., 16
Differences. *See* Diversity
Discipline
    decent immigrant narrative and, 31
    ethnic credits and racial penalties and, 31
    stigma against Black schools and, 78, 79,
        82–84
Discontents of diversity, 58–60
Distributed Leadership Study (DLS), 4,
    113
Diversity
    alternate approach to, 108–11
    balancing the costs and benefits of, 61
    as benefit to dominant group, 44
    benefits of, 1, 7, 43, 44, 53–58, 107–108
    discontents of, 47, 58–60
    dividing up, 4, 7–21, 89
    as dominant form for thinking about
        minorities, 1
    fulfilling the promise of, 5, 107–111
    judging good and bad, 5, 43–61
    as leaving Black schools behind, 84–85
    purpose of embracing, 8
    racial conflict as by-product of, 58
    as reinforcing old racial hierarchies, 21
    ritually praising, 49–51
    shortcomings of, 108
    teachers valuing of, 107
    teaching about, 53–54
    unintended consequences of, 1–2
    See also specific topic
Diversity discourse
    dividing up differences and, 2, 10
    ethnic differences and, 84–85
    racial hierarchy and, 2
    racism and, 2
    ritual praise of diversity and, 49–51
    stigma against Black schools and, 2,
        84–85
Dixson, A., 108
Dodge Elementary School (multiracial
    school)
    benefits of teaching at, 7, 46–47

demographics of, 20, 45–46, 52–53
and first experiences teaching at Black schools, 67
good and bad diversity and, 43, 44–53, 54–56, 57–58, 59–60
how teachers came to teach at, 47–48
influence of diversity on teachers at, 43
Laketown demographics and, 44–45
as multiracial oasis in segregated city, 44–46
promise of diversity and, 109
reputation of, 45
teacher demographics at, 21
White norm and, 87, 89, 90–91, 92, 95, 96–97, 98–99, 102–104
See also specific topic
DuBois, W.E.B., 63

Education
Americanization as goal of, 91
valuing of, 30, 37, 97, 101
Ehrenberg, R., 14
Embrick, D., 10, 114
Empathy/sympathy, 36–37, 38, 42
Entwisle, D., 16, 23, 46
Environment. *See* Climate
Equality/inequality
avoiding discussions about, 3
dividing up differences and, 8, 17, 18
ethnicizing minority status and, 17
good and bad diversity and, 59
orthodox inequality and, 109–111
productive diversity and, 18
promise of diversity and, 108, 109–111
stigma against Black schools and, 81
Erving Elementary School (Black school), 20, 21, 64, 73–74
Esser, H., 98
Ethnic credits
in the classroom, 23–42
dividing up differences and, 9, 10
ethnic narratives and, 24–32, 33
racial hierarchy and, 2

racial narratives and, 24–25, 32–40
social cost of minority status and, 41–42
WCTs and Frustrated Natives and, 40–41
White norm and, 96, 97, 102–103, 105, 106
Ethnic harmony, good and bad diversity and, 58
Ethnic labels, 113
Ethnic narratives, 23–32
See also specific narrative
Ethnicity
definition of, 2
diversity discourse and, 84–85
history of, 10–14
privileging of, 2
promise of diversity and, 109–11
sources of, 25
stigma against Black schools and, 84–85
White norm and, 88–90
See also specific topic
Exceptionally good, Black schools as, 5, 72–74
Expectations
at-risk kids narrative and, 37
dividing up differences and, 8, 15
ethnic credits and racial penalties and, 24, 29, 37, 38, 41
immigrant status as burden narrative and, 29
social cost of minority status and, 41
social responsibility narrative and, 28
stigma against Black schools and, 65, 66, 73–74, 83
teacher perceptions of minority students and, 15
of White teachers by Blacks, 71

Failure, stigma against Black schools and, 63, 65, 66, 78
Farkas, G., 14
Farley, J. E., 11
Fass, P. S., 11, 12, 13

Ferguson, R. F., 14, 16
Fordham, S., 65
Foster Elementary School (Black school), 20, 21, 64, 66, 68, 81–82
Foster, M., 37, 38
Four Musketeers story, 57
Francis, B., 14
Frankenberg, E., 5, 15, 21, 46, 93, 108, 113
Fraser, Lady Antonia, 3
Freeman, D. J., 16, 67
Frustrated Natives, 40, 41

Gallagher, C., 10, 24, 89, 110
Garner, R., 88
Gay, G., 80
Gender
    culture of poverty narratives and, 34–35
    White norm and, 95–96
Generational issues, social responsibility narrative and, 41
Gifted programs, 100–101
Goffman, E., 65
Grant Elementary School (Black school), 51
Grobe, R. P., 14
Groulx, J. G., 15, 107
Guglielmo, T. A., 12

Hartmann, D., 5, 10, 47
Hill High School (Black school), 67
Hollingsworth, S., 5, 18, 44
Hsu, R. Y., 8, 17, 24, 85

Ideology
    dividing up differences and, 17
    See also specific ideology
Immigrant minorities
    dividing up differences and, 9
    as embodiment of American Dream, 85
    hierarchy of, 2
    stereotypes of, 108
    See also White ethnic immigrants; *specific minority or topic*

Immigrant status as burden narrative, 26, 27–30
Instruction. *See* Teaching

Jacobson, M. F., 12, 92
James, D., 5, 18, 44
Jamieson, F., 5, 18, 44
Jim Crow racism, 107
Johnson, M. F., 99–100
Jung, M.-K., 18

"Kids are just kids" strategy, stigma against Black schools and, 72, 75–78
Kim, C. J., 2, 9, 10, 19
Kipps Elementary School (Black school), 20, 21, 64, 65–66, 72–73, 75, 76, 81, 82, 84

Ladson-Billings, G., 17, 37, 108
Laketown
    overview of, 18–21
    segregation in, 18–21, 44, 71
    theorizing racial orthodoxy in, 16–18
    See also specific school
Laketown Public Schools (LPS), 67, 69, 71
Language
    at-risk kids narrative and, 36
    as barrier, 27–30, 36, 41
    ethnic credits and racial penalties and, 27–30, 36, 41
    immigrant status as burden narrative and, 27–30
    social cost of minority status and, 41
    White norm and, 89, 90
    See also Bilingualism
Latino schools
    characteristics of Lakewood, 20
    racial hierarchy and, 2–3
    teacher perceptions of, 2–3, 107
    White norm and, 105
    See also Putnam Elementary School; Stanley Elementary School

Latinos
  dividing up differences and, 2
  as DSL teachers, 21, 113
  See also specific topic or school
Lee, J., 108, 111
Lewis, A., 114
"Lift as we climb" ethos, 39
Loadman, W. E., 16, 67

Mainstream, White norm and, 5, 93–99
Margolin, L., 100, 101
Martin Elementary School (Black school),
    20, 21, 64, 69–70, 71, 74, 77, 80, 83,
    103
McBride, D., 91
McCarthy, C., 17
Middle class, White norm and, 5, 87, 88,
    94–95, 99–106
Minorities
  distinguishing between, 51–53
  dividing up differences and, 14–16, 17
  ethnicizing minority status and, 17
  good and bad diversity and, 51–53
  hierarchy of, 1, 2, 51–53
  "model minorities" and, 17
  and social cost of minority status, 41–42
  stereotypes of, 108
  stigma against Black schools and, 85
  teacher perceptions of, 14–16
  See also Immigrant minorities; *specific
      minority*
Minority schools, definition of, 113
Morality
  culture of poverty narratives and, 25, 27,
      32, 33
  decent immigrants narrative and, 30–32
  ethnic credits and racial penalties and,
      23, 24, 25, 27, 30–32, 33, 41
  social cost of minority status and, 41
  White norm and, 88
Mueller, C. W., 16, 70
Multicultural capital, 5, 18, 40, 44, 54–55,
    58, 60

Multiculturalism
  dividing up differences and, 8, 17, 18
  good and bad diversity and, 44, 48–49,
      51, 53–54, 57, 58, 59, 61
  immigrant status as burden narrative
      and, 27–28
  multiracial schools and, 44, 48–49, 51,
      53–54, 57, 58, 59, 61, 63, 84
  productive diversity and, 18
  promise of diversity and, 107
  shortcomings of, 1, 3
  as social norm, 48–49, 51
  stigma against Black schools and, 84
  teachers response to diversity and, 1
  theorizing racial orthodoxy in Laketown
      and, 17
  See also Colorblind multiculturalism
Multiracial schools
  adjustment of teaching at, 80
  benefits of, 2, 5, 43
  celebrations of students' heritages at,
      81, 84
  characteristics of Lakewood, 20
  cosmopolitanism at, 48–53
  definition of, 113
  desirability of teaching in, 1, 2, 5, 61
  as embodying America's ideals, 63
  enrollments in, 64
  good and bad diversity and, 43–61, 85
  how teachers came to teach at, 47–48
  judging difference in, 43–61
  outside world response to diversity of,
      49, 50–51
  promise of diversity and, 109
  racial hierarchy and, 2
  recruitment of minorites for, 52
  as representative of America's future, 63
  as socially valuable, 61
  teachers attraction to, 1, 5, 9, 43, 45,
      46–47, 73, 75, 78
  tolerance at, 44, 48–53, 56, 59, 61, 63,
      78, 81
  United Nations analogy for, 46

Multiracial schools (*continued*)
  White norm and, 105
  See also Bowen Elementary School;
    Dodge Elementary School; *specific*
    topic
Myers, K. A., 8

Narratives
  ethnic, 23–25, 26, 32–40, 114
  racial, 23–32, 114
  See also specific narrative
Native Americans, 9, 11, 13, 24
Neckerman, K., 108, 111
Neighborhood. *See* community
New London Group, 18, 43
Nieto, S., 110
Noel Elementary School (Black school),
    20, 21, 66, 76

O'Connor, C., 9
Ogbu, J., 9, 14, 65
Olneck, M. R., 49
Omi, M., 2, 8, 24
"Other"
  dividing up differences and, 18
  learning about, 54–55
  in multiracial schools, 78
  perpetuating White normativity and, 18

Parents/families
  at-risk kids narratives and, 35–37
  culture of poverty narratives and, 26, 27,
    33–34
  decent immigrants narrative and, 30–32
  dividing up differences and, 9
  ethnic credits and racial penalties and,
    4–5, 25, 26, 27, 28, 29, 30–32,
    33–34, 35–37, 38–39, 41, 42
  extended, 32, 90
  good and bad diversity and, 52
  immigrant status as burden and, 28, 29,
    30
  involvement of, 4–5, 9, 25, 29, 30, 35–37,

    41, 87, 94–95, 99, 101–103, 105,
    111
  language barriers and, 28, 29
  in multiracial schools, 52
  promise of diversity and, 111
  social cost of minority status and, 41, 42
  social responsibility narrative and, 38–39
  stigma against Black schools and, 83
  White norm and, 87, 88, 90, 94–96, 99,
    101–103, 105
Perry, P., 87, 102
Pierre, J., 8, 23, 24, 42
Pluralism
  dividing up differences and, 11–12, 13,
    17
  good and bad diversity and, 53, 55–58,
    61
  history of race and ethnicity and, 11–12,
    13
  in multiracial schools, 53, 55–58, 61, 78
  promise of diversity and, 107
  and proving that pluralism works,
    55–58, 61
  theorizing racial orthodoxy in Laketown
    and, 17
Politics, promise of diversity and, 109
Pollock, M., 8, 59
Poverty
  at-risk kids narrative and, 37
  ethnic credits and racial penalties and,
    23, 30, 32, 37, 42
  good and bad diversity and, 52
  promise of diversity and, 111
  social costs of, 32, 42
  stigma against Black schools and, 64
  See also Culture of poverty narrative
Power
  diversity discourse and, 10
  dividing up differences and, 8, 10, 17
  ethnic credits and racial penalties and,
    24–25
  ethnicizing minority status and, 17
  promise of diversity and, 108, 109–10

Pre-service teachers, perceptions of
  minority students of, 14–15
Price, J. L., 16, 70
Productive diversity
  benefiting from diversity and, 53–58
  good and bad diversity and, 43–44, 47,
    53–54, 58, 61
  in multiracial schools, 43–44, 47, 53–54,
    58, 61, 78, 84
  promise of diversity and, 107–108
  stigma against Black schools and, 63–64,
    78, 84
  White norm and, 88
Putnam Elementary School (Latino
  school), 20, 21, 93, 94, 95, 103

Race
  avoiding discussions about, 3
  definition of, 1–2
  diversity as reinforcing old racial
    hierarchies and, 21
  history of, 10–14
  promise of diversity and, 109–111
  See also specific topic
Racial code words, 14, 47, 48, 51, 113
Racial discourse
  dividing up differences and, 7–8, 10
  good and bad diversity and, 61
  as political, 8
  proper, 7
  silences and, 7–8
Racial harmony
  good and bad diversity and, 46, 55–58,
    60, 61
  multiracial schools and, 46, 55–58, 60,
    61, 63
Racial hierarchy
  dividing up differences and, 2, 8
  promise of diversity and, 111
  stigma against Black schools and, 76
  triangulation of, 2, 9–10, 15, 19
  White norm and, 93
Racial labels, 93, 99, 113

Racial narratives
  of teachers, 23–25, 26, 32–40
  See also specific narrative
Racial penalties
  in the classroom, 23–42
  dividing up differences and, 9, 10
  ethnic narratives and, 23–32, 33
  racial hierarchy and, 2
  racial narratives and, 23–25, 26, 32–40
  social cost of minority status and,
    41–42
  WCTs and Frustrated Natives and,
    40–41
Racism
  diversity discourse and, 2
  dividing up differences and, 8
  promise of diversity and, 108, 110
  teachers response to diviersity and, 1
Randolph, Antonia Maria, 3–4
Reay, D., 5, 18, 44
Rehabilitative ethnicity, 8
Religion, White norm and, 88, 98–99
Resilience, 29, 109, 111
Rewards. *See* Ethnic credits; Symbolic
  rewards
Rist, R., 15
Ritual praise of diversity, 48–51
Role models, 39
Rosenbloom, S.R., 14, 107
Rousseau, C., 108

Schools
  as arena for racial struggle, 110
  climate of, 15–16
  as "filling in the gap," 29
  function of public, 11
  as tools for social democracy, 11
  United Nations comparison with, 7
  See also specific school
Segregation
  good and bad diversity and, 48, 59
  history of race and ethnicity and, 13
  in Laketown, 19

Segregation (*continued*)
  stigma against Black schools and, 63, 64,
    69, 71, 85
Self-fulfilling prophecy, 15–16
Shapiro, T. M., 99–100
Sheehan, D., 14
Shuan, Y., 14
Sleeter, C. E., 15, 110
Social class
  at-risk kids narrative and, 36–37
  ethnic credits and racial penalties and,
    36–37, 41, 42
  promise of diversity and, 111
  social cost of minority status and, 42
  social responsibility narrative and, 41
  See also Social mobility
Social costs
  of minority status, 41–42
  of poverty, 32
Social hierarchies, assimilating diversity
  and, 109–11
Social justice
  and diversity as dominant form for
    thinking about minorities, 1
  dividing up differences and, 4, 18
  ethnic credits and racial penalties and,
    37, 38
  productive diversity and, 18
  promise of diversity and, 5, 108, 110,
    111
  social responsibility narrative and, 37, 38
Social mobility, 39, 41, 42
Social norm, multiculturalism as, 48–49, 51
Social responsibility narrative, 25, 27,
  37–40, 42
The Souls of Black Folk (DuBois), 63
Spillane, J., 16
Splitting, stigma against Black schools
  and, 72
Standardized tests, 60
Stanley Elementary School (Latino
  school), 20, 21, 89, 95, 105, 107, 108,
  109, 110

Stuart Elementary School (White school),
  76
Students
  as caring, 31
  deficits of, 78–80
  empowerment of, 81–82
  teachers' long-term investment in, 39–40
  See also specific topic
Suburban schools, 15, 77, 83, 99, 102,
  103–5
Symbolic burden of teaching at Black
  schools, 65–66, 72–78
"Symbolic currency," 24
Symbolic resources, ethnic credits and
  racial penalties and, 24, 41
Symbolic rewards, definition of, 9
Sympathy/empathy, 36–37, 38, 42

Teachers
  authority of, 31
  branding of Black school, 65
  long-term investment in students of,
    39–40
  perceptions of minority students of,
    14–16, 19
  personal experiences with race of, 48
  recruitment and retention of, 15, 16
  See also specific topic
Teaching
  accommodation of teaching to diversity,
    43, 53, 61
  adjustment at multiracial schools, 80
  creative, 80
  culturally relevant pedagogy and, 78,
    80–81, 82, 107
  dividing up differences and, 15–16
  good and bad diversity and, 43, 53, 58,
    61
  promise of diversity and, 107–8, 110
  stigma against Black schools and, 78–84
  symbolic burden of teaching at Black
    schools and, 65–66, 72–78
Thompson, M. S., 16, 23, 46

Tolerance
    good and bad diversity and, 44, 53, 56,
        59, 61
    in multiracial schools, 44, 48–53, 56, 59,
        61, 63, 78, 81
    promise of diversity and, 107, 108, 110
    teaching about, 53–54
Tri-racial hierarchy, 2, 9–10, 15, 19
Trips, taking students on, 39, 40
Tyack, D., 10, 11, 12, 13, 17, 55, 107

United Nations analogy, 7, 46
United States, self-perception of, 18
University School (middle-class school),
    103
Urban schools, 15, 103–4, 105, 106

Values
    achievement and, 29, 30
    culture of poverty narrative and, 32
    decent immigrants narrative and, 30–32
    dividing up differences and, 15
    ethnic credits and racial penalties and,
        23, 24, 29, 30–32, 42
    immigrant status as burden narrative
        and, 29, 30
    social cost of minority status and, 42
    teacher perceptions of minority students
        and, 15
    White norm and, 88, 90
Violence
    culture of poverty narratives and, 26,
        27, 33
    social cost of minority status and, 41
    stigma against Black schools and, 5, 65
    See also Danger

Walters, P. B., 38
Warikoo, N., 19
Watts Elementary School (Black school),
    20, 21, 64, 69, 71, 74, 77, 81, 82–83,
    84
Way, N., 14, 107

Well-meaning Cultural Tourists (WCTs),
    40–41
White dominance/supremacy
    dividing up differences and, 8, 10
    social cost of minority status and, 42
    teachers embrace of diversity and, 8
White ethnic immigrants
    historical treatment of, 11–13
    as model for understanding how to
        address social diversity, 11
    White norm and, 88–90, 91–92
    See also specific topic
White norm
    achievement and, 87, 99, 100–101, 103
    advantages of, 5, 87–88
    American-ness and, 5, 90–93
    assimilating diversity and, 4, 88
    assimilation and, 88, 90–93, 95
    colorblind multiculturalism, 91
    culture and, 90–99
    dividing up diversity and, 89
    ethnic credits and, 96, 97, 102–3, 105,
        106
    ethnicity and, 88–90
    mainstream and, 5, 93–99
    middle class and, 5, 87, 88, 94–95,
        99–106
    parents/families and, 87, 88, 90, 94–96,
        99, 101–3, 105
    preserving the, 18, 87–106
    promise of diversity and, 108, 111
    religion and, 88, 98–99
    White immigrants and, 88–90
White teachers
    Black expectations of, 71
    outsider status of, 70–71
    stigma against Black schools and, 65–66,
        69, 70–71, 72, 84
    See also specific topic
Williams, K., 5, 18, 44
Williamson, P., 8
Winant, H., 2, 8, 24
World War II, 13, 92

About the Author

Antonia Randolph is an assistant professor of sociology at the University of Delaware. She has been published in journals such as *Anthropology and Education Quarterly* and *Youth and Society*.